SHAKESPEARE MADE EASY

Modern version side-by-side with full original text

A Midsummer Night's Dream

Edited and rendered into modern English by
Alan Durband

Hutchinson

London Melbourne Sydney Auckland Johannesburg

Hutchinson Education

An imprint of Century Hutchinson Ltd
62-65 Chandos Place, London WC2N 4NW

Century Hutchinson Australia (Pty) Ltd
PO Box 496, 16-22 Church Street, Hawthorn,
Victoria 3122, Australia

Century Hutchinson New Zealand Ltd
PO Box 40-086, 32-34 View Road, Glenfield,
Auckland 10, New Zealand

Century Hutchinson South Africa (Pty) Ltd
PO Box 337, Bergvlei 2012, South Africa

First published 1984
Reprinted 1985, 1987, 1988
© Alan Durband 1984

Photoset in Plantin and Univers by
Colset Pte. Ltd, Singapore

Printed and bound in Great Britain by
The Guernsey Press Co. Ltd., Guernsey, Channel Islands

British Library Cataloguing in Publication Data

Shakespeare, William
    A midsummer night's dream.——(Shakespeare made easy)
    I. Title   II. Durband, Alan   III. Series
    822.3'3   PR2827

ISBN 0 09 172910 6

'Reade him therefore: and againe, and againe: And if then you do not like him, surely you are in some danger, not to understand him . . . .'

John Hemming
Henry Condell

Preface to the 1623 Folio Edition

Shakespeare Made Easy

Other drama books edited by Alan Durband

Contents

Introduction

Shakespeare Made Easy is intended for readers approaching the plays for the first time, who find the language of Elizabethan poetic drama an initial obstacle to understanding and enjoyment. In the past, the only answer to the problem has been to grapple with the difficulties with the aid of explanatory footnotes (often missing when they are most needed) and a stern teacher. Generations of students have complained that 'Shakespeare was ruined for me at school'.

Usually a fuller appreciation of Shakespeare's plays comes in later life. Often the desire to read Shakespeare for pleasure and enrichment follows from a visit to the theatre, where excellence of acting and production can bring to life qualities which sometimes lie dormant on the printed page.

Shakespeare Made Easy can never be a substitute for the original plays. It cannot possibly convey the full meaning of Shakespeare's poetic expression, which is untranslatable. *Shakespeare Made Easy* concentrates on the dramatic aspect, enabling the novice to become familiar with the plot and characters, and to experience one facet of Shakespeare's genius. To know and understand the central issues of each play is a sound starting point for further exploration and development.

Discretion can be used in choosing the best method to employ. One way is to read the original Shakespeare first, ignoring the modern version – or using it only when interest or understanding flags. Another way is to read the translation first, to establish confidence and familiarity with plot and characters.

Either way, cross-reference can be illuminating. The modern text can explain 'what is being said' if Shakespeare's language is particularly complex or his expression antiquated. The Shakespeare text will show the reader of the modern paraphrase how much more can be expressed in poetry than in prose.

The use of *Shakespeare Made Easy* means that the newcomer need never be overcome by textual difficulties. From first to last, a measure of understanding is at hand – the key is provided for what has been a locked door to many students in the past. And as understanding grows, so an awareness develops of the potential of language as a vehicle for philosophic and moral expression, beauty, and the abidingly memorable.

Even professional Shakespearian scholars can never hope to arrive at a complete understanding of the plays. Each critic, researcher, actor or producer merely adds a little to the work that has already been done, or makes fresh interpretations of the texts for new generations. For everyone, Shakespearian appreciation is a journey. *Shakespeare Made Easy* is intended to help with the first steps.

William Shakespeare

His life

William Shakespeare was born in Stratford-on-Avon, Warwickshire, on 23 April 1564, the son of a prosperous wool and leather merchant. Very little is known of his early life. From parish records we know that he married Ann Hathaway in 1582, when he was eighteen, and she was twenty-six. They had three children, the eldest of whom died in childhood.

Between his marriage and the next thing we know about him, there is a gap of ten years. Probably he became a member of a travelling company of actors. By 1592 he had settled in London, and had earned a reputation as an actor and playwright.

Theatres were then in their infancy. The first (called *The Theatre*) was built in 1576. Two more followed as the taste for theatre grew: *The Curtain* in 1577 and *The Rose* in 1587. The demand for new plays naturally increased. Shakespeare probably earned a living adapting old plays and working in collaboration with others on new ones. Today we would call him a 'freelance', since he was not permanently attached to one theatre.

In 1594, a new company of actors, The Lord Chamberlain's Men was formed, and Shakespeare was one of the shareholders. He remained a member throughout his working life. The company regrouped in 1603, and was re-named The King's Men, with James I as their patron.

Shakespeare and his fellow-actors prospered. In 1598 they built their own theatre, *The Globe*, which broke away from the traditional rectangular shape of the inn and its yard (the early home of travelling bands of actors). Shakespeare described it in *Henry V* as 'this wooden O', because it was circular.

Many other theatres were built by investors eager to profit from the new enthusiasm for drama. *The Hope*, *The Fortune*,

The Red Bull and *The Swan* were all open-air 'public' theatres. There were also many 'private' (or indoor) theatres, one of which (*The Blackfriars*) was purchased by Shakespeare and his friends because the child actors who performed there were dangerous competitors. (Shakespeare denounces them in *Hamlet*.)

After writing some thirty-seven plays (the exact number is something which scholars argue about), Shakespeare retired to his native Stratford, wealthy and respected. He died on his birthday, in 1616.

His plays

Shakespeare's plays were not all published in his lifetime. None of them comes to us exactly as he wrote it.

In Elizabethan times, plays were not regarded as either literature or good reading matter. They were written at speed (often by more than one writer), performed perhaps ten or twelve times, and then discarded. Fourteen of Shakespeare's plays were first printed in Quarto (17cm × 21cm) volumes, not all with his name as the author. Some were authorized (the 'good' Quartos) and probably were printed from prompt copies provided by the theatre. Others were pirated (the 'bad' Quartos) by booksellers who may have employed shorthand writers, or bought actors' copies after the run of the play had ended.

In 1623, seven years after Shakespeare's death, John Hemming and Henry Condell (fellow-actors and shareholders in The King's Men) published a collected edition of Shakespeare's works – thirty-six plays in all – in a Folio (21cm × 34cm) edition. From their introduction it would seem that they used Shakespeare's original manuscripts ('we have scarce received from him a blot in his papers') but the Folio volumes that still survive are not all exactly alike, nor are the plays printed as we know them today, with act and scene divisions and stage-directions.

A modern edition of a Shakespeare play is the result of a great deal of scholarly research and editorial skill over several centuries. The aim is always to publish a text (based on the good and bad Quartos and the Folio editions) that most closely resembles what Shakespeare intended. Misprints have added to the problems, so some words and lines are pure guesswork. This explains why some versions of Shakespeare's plays differ from others.

His theatre

The first purpose-built playhouse in Elizabethan London, constructed in 1576, was *The Theatre*. Its co-founders were John Brayne, an investor, and James Burbage, a carpenter turned actor. Like the six or seven 'public' (or outdoor) theatres which followed it over the next thirty years, it was situated outside the city, to avoid conflict with the authorities. They disapproved of players and playgoing, partly on moral and political grounds, and partly because of the danger of spreading the plague. (There were two major epidemics during Shakespeare's lifetime, and on each occasion the theatres were closed for lengthy periods.)

The Theatre was a financial success, and Shakespeare's company performed there until 1598, when a dispute over the lease of the land forced Burbage to take down the building. It was re-created in Southwark, as *The Globe*, with Shakespeare and several of his fellow-actors as the principal shareholders.

By modern standards, *The Globe* was small. Externally, the octagonal building measured less than thirty metres across, but in spite of this it could accommodate an audience of between two and three thousand people. (The largest of the three theatres at the National Theatre complex in London today seats 1160.)

Performances were advertised by means of playbills posted around the city, and they took place during the hours of daylight when the weather was suitable. A flag flew to show that all was well, to save playgoers a wasted journey.

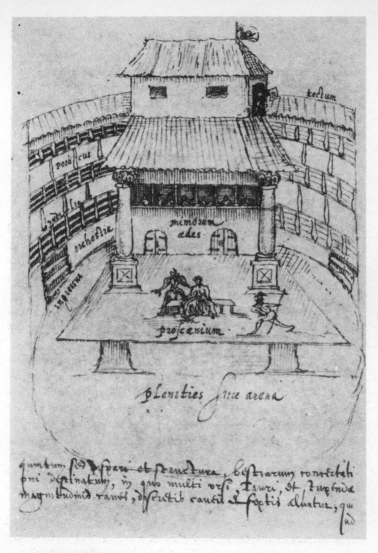

Interior of the Swan Theatre – from a pen and ink drawing made in 1596 (Mansell Collection)

At the entrance, a doorkeeper collected one penny (about 60p in modern money) for admission to the 'pit' – a name taken from the old inn-yards, where bear-baiting and cock-fighting were popular sports. This was the minimum charge for seeing a play. The 'groundlings', as they were called, simply stood around the three sides of the stage, in the open air. Those who were better off could pay extra for a seat under cover. Stairs led from the pit to three tiers of galleries round the walls. The higher one went, the more one paid. The best seats cost one shilling (or £6 today). In theatres owned by speculators like Francis Langley and Philip Henslowe, half the gallery takings went to the landlord.

A full house might consist of 800 groundlings and 1500 in the galleries, with a dozen more exclusive seats on the stage itself for the gentry. A new play might run for between six and sixteen performances; the average was about ten. As there were no breaks between scenes, and no intervals, most plays could be performed in two hours. A trumpet sounded three times before the play began.

The acting company assembled in the Tiring House at the rear of the stage. This was where they 'attired' (or dressed) themselves: not in costumes representing the period of the play, but in Elizabethan doublet and hose. All performances were therefore in modern dress, though no expense was spared to make the stage costumes lavish. The entire company was male. By law actresses were not allowed, and female roles were performed by boys.

Access to the stage from the Tiring House was through two doors, one on each side of the stage. Because there was no front curtain, every entrance had to have its corresponding exit, so an actor killed on stage had to be carried off. There was no scenery: the audience used its imagination, guided by the spoken word. Storms and night scenes might well be performed on sunny days in mid-afternoon; the Elizabethan playgoer relied entirely on the playwright's descriptive skills to establish the dramatic atmosphere.

Once on stage, the actors and their expensive clothes were protected from sudden showers by a canopy, the underside of which was painted blue, and spangled with stars to represent the heavens. A trapdoor in the stage made ghostly entrances and the gravedigging scene in *Hamlet* possible. Behind the main stage, in between the two entrance doors, there was a curtained area, concealing a small inner stage, useful for bedroom scenes. Above this was a balcony, which served for castle walls (as in *Henry V*) or a domestic balcony (as in the famous scene in *Romeo and Juliet*).

The acting style in Elizabethan times was probably more declamatory than we favour today, but the close proximity of the audience also made a degree of intimacy possible. In those days soliloquies and asides seemed quite natural. Act and scene divisions did not exist (those in printed versions of the play today have been added by editors), but Shakespeare often indicates a scene-ending by a rhyming couplet.

A company such as The King's Men at *The Globe* would consist of around twenty-five actors, half of whom might be shareholders, and the rest part-timers engaged for a particular play. Amongst the shareholders in *The Globe* were several specialists – William Kempe, for example, was a renowned comedian and Robert Armin was a singer and dancer. Playwrights wrote parts to suit the actors who were available, and devised ways of overcoming the absence of women. Shakespeare often has his heroines dress as young men, and physical contact between lovers was formal compared with the realism we expect today.

His verse

Shakespeare wrote his plays mostly in blank verse: that is, unrhymed lines consisting of ten syllables, alternately stressed and unstressed. The technical term for this form is the 'iambic pentameter'. When Shakespeare first began to write for the

13

stage, it was fashionable to maintain this regular beat from the first line of the play till the last.

Shakespeare conformed at first, and then experimented. Some of his early plays contain whole scenes in rhyming couplets – in *Romeo and Juliet*, for example, there is extensive use of rhyme, and as if to show his versatility, Shakespeare even inserts a sonnet into the dialogue.

But as he matured, he sought greater freedom of expression than rhyme allowed. Rhyme is still used to indicate a scene-ending, or to stress lines which he wishes the audience to remember. Generally, though, Shakespeare moved towards the rhythms of everyday speech. This gave him many dramatic advantages, which he fully and subtly exploits in terms of atmosphere, character, emotion, stress and pace.

It is Shakespeare's poetic imagery, however, that most distinguishes his verse from that of lesser playwrights. It enables him to stretch the imagination, express complex thought-patterns in memorable language, and convey a number of associated ideas in a compressed and economical form. A study of Shakespeare's imagery – especially in his later plays – is often the key to a full understanding of his meaning and purposes.

At the other extreme is prose. Shakespeare normally reserves it for servants, clowns, commoners, and pedestrian matters such as lists, messages and letters.

A Midsummer Night's Dream

Date

A Midsummer Night's Dream was first published in 1600 in a Quarto edition, probably from Shakespeare's manuscript rather than a prompt copy. It was written several years earlier, about 1595, and may well have been commissioned for performance at an important wedding.

Source

This is one of the few Shakespearian plays which has no single identifiable source. It is not a re-working of an older play, or a dramatisation of a particular story already in print. The origins of some of the characters and plot are traceable to a variety of works which would have formed part of Shakespeare's general reading. North's *Plutarch*, Chaucer's *Knight's Tale* and *Legend of Good Women*, Golding's translation of Ovid's *Metamorphoses*, Adlington's translation of *The Golden Ass* of Apuleius, Montemayor's *Diana* are some of the many literary sources which scholars have identified. In all probability, Shakespeare wrote the play as an original piece, his inspiration having the benefit of a well-read man's range and sensibility.

Text

Scholars are satisfied that the first Quarto edition of 1600 can be trusted as definitive, that is, as the most accurate version of what Shakespeare actually wrote.

A Midsummer Night's Dream

Original text and modern version

The Characters

Theseus   duke of Athens
Hippolyta   queen of the Amazons, betrothed to Theseus
Lysander ⎫
Demetrius ⎭ in love with Hermia
Hermia   in love with Lysander
Helena   in love with Demetrius
Egeus   Hermia's father
Philostrate   the duke's master of revels
Peter Quince   a carpenter
Nick Bottom   a weaver
Francis Flute   a bellows-mender
Tom Snout   a tinker
Robin Starveling   a tailor
Snug   a joiner
Oberon   king of the fairies
Titania   queen of the fairies
Puck   (Robin Goodfellow) Oberon's lieutenant
A Fairy   servant to Titania
Peaseblossom
Cobweb ⎫
Moth ⎬ fairies in the service of Titania
Mustardseed ⎭
Attendant fairies, Lords and Attendants to Theseus and Hippolyta, Huntsmen.

Act one

Scene 1

Athens. Enter **Theseus, Hippolyta, Philostrate** *and* **Attendants.**

Theseus Now, fair Hippolyta, our nuptial hour
Draws on apace; four happy days bring in
Another moon: but O, methinks how slow
This old moon wanes! She lingers my desires
5 Like to a step-dame or a dowager,
Long withering out a young man's revenue.

Hippolyta Four days will quickly steep themselves in night;
Four nights will quickly dream away the time;
10 And then the moon, like to a silver bow
New bent in heaven, shall behold the night
Of our solemnities.

Theseus Go, Philostrate,
Stir up the Athenian youth to merriments;
15 Awake the pert and nimble spirit of mirth;
Turn melancholy forth to funerals;
The pale companion is not for our pomp.

[*Exit* **Philostrate**]

Hippolyta, I wooed thee with my sword,
And won thy love doing thee injuries;
20 But I will wed thee in another key,
With pomp, with triumph, and with revelling.

Act one

Scene 1

Athens. Enter **Theseus, Hippolyta, Philostrate** *and* **Attendants.**

Theseus   Our wedding day will soon be here, dear Hippolyta. Four happy days from now a new moon rises. How slowly this old moon wanes! She makes time drag: like when a long-lived stepmother or a widow, keeps a young man waiting for his inheritance!

Hippolyta   Four days will quickly merge into night, and we'll quickly dream four nights away. Then the moon, resembling a silver bow newly bent in the sky, will witness the night of our celebrations.

Theseus   Go, Philostrate. Get the youth of Athens in a merry mood. Rouse up the spirit of quick-witted mirth. Send mournfulness to funerals. We want no dreary people at our nuptials.

[**Philostrate** *exits*]

Hippolyta, I wooed you as a conqueror, and won your love through victory over you. But I shall marry you in a different manner – with spectacle, festivity, and rejoicing.

[*Enter* **Egeus** *and* **Hermia** *his daughter*, **Lysander**, *and*
Demetrius]

Egeus   Happy be Theseus, our renowned Duke!

Theseus   Thanks, good Egeus: what's the news with thee?

Egeus   Full of vexation come I, with complaint
25   Against my child, my daughter Hermia.
Stand forth, Demetrius. My noble lord,
This man hath my consent to marry her.
Stand forth, Lysander; and, my gracious Duke,
This man hath bewitched the bosom of my child:
30   Thou, thou Lysander, thou hast given her rhymes,
And interchanged love-tokens with my child:
Thou hast by moonlight at her window sung,
With feigning voice verses of feigning love,
And stolen the impression of her fantasy
35   With bracelets of thy hair, rings, gawds, conceits,
Knacks, trifles, nosegays, sweetmeats, messengers
Of strong prevailment in unhardened youth;
With cunning hast thou filched my daughter's heart,
Turned her obedience, which is due to me,
40   To stubborn harshness. And, my gracious Duke,
Be it so she will not here before your grace
Consent to marry with Demetrius,
I beg the ancient privilege of Athens:
As she is mine, I may dispose of her;
45   Which shall be either to this gentleman,
Or to her death, according to our law
Immediately provided in that case.

Theseus   What say you, Hermia? Be advised, fair maid.
To you your father should be as a god:
50   One that composed your beauties; yea, and one
To whom you are but as a form in wax

[**Egeus** *enters, with his daughter* **Hermia**, *followed by*
Lysander *and* **Demetrius**]

Egeus All happiness to Theseus, our distinguished Duke!

Theseus Thanks, good Egeus. How are things with you?

Egeus I have come to you as a father in distress, furious
with my daughter Hermia. Demetrius – step forward. My
noble lord, this man has my consent to marry her.
Lysander – step forward. This one, my gracious Duke,
has infatuated her. You, Lysander – you! – have given
her poems, and exchanged love-tokens with my child.
You have serenaded her at her window by moonlight,
crooning songs of so-called love. You've turned her head
with bracelets made from your hair, and rings, and
ribbons, and baubles, knick-knacks, presents, posies
and confectionery – all very influential with the
immature. Very cleverly you've stolen her heart, and
turned the obedience I'm entitled to into stubborn
wilfulness. And, my gracious Duke, if she will not agree
– here, in front of your grace – to marry Demetrius, then
I beg my ancient Athenian right. As she is my daughter I
can decide her fate. She shall either marry this gentleman
[*indicating* **Demetrius**] or she shall die, according to the
law that's applicable in such cases.

Theseus What do you say to this, Hermia? I'll give you a
word of advice, fair maid. To you, your father should be
like a god. He gave you your beauty. Indeed, to him you
are a figure he has stamped in wax, his to let be or

By him imprinted; and within his power
To leave the figure, or disfigure it.
Demetrius is a worthy gentleman.

Hermia   So is Lysander.

55 **Theseus**   In himself he is;
But in this kind, wanting your father's voice,
The other must be held the worthier.

Hermia   I would my father looked but with my eyes.

Theseus   Rather your eyes must with his judgement look.

60 **Hermia**   I do entreat your Grace to pardon me.
I know not by what power I am made bold,
Nor how it may concern my modesty
In such a presence here to plead my thought;
But I beseech your Grace, that I may know
65 The worst that may befall me in this case,
If I refuse to wed Demetrius.

Theseus   Either to die the death, or to abjure
For ever the society of men.
Therefore, fair Hermia, question your desires,
70 Know of your youth, examine well your blood,
Whether, if you yield not to your father's choice,
You can endure the livery of a nun,
For aye to be in shady cloister mewed,
To live a barren sister all your life,
75 Chanting faint hymns to the cold fruitless moon.
Thrice blessed they that master so their blood
To undergo such maiden pilgrimage;
But earthlier happy is the rose distilled
Than that which, withering on the virgin thorn,
80 Grows, lives, and dies in single blessedness.

destroy. Demetrius is a worthy gentleman.

Hermia   So is Lysander.

Theseus   Seen on his own, apart from these events, he is. But in matters of this kind, since he lacks your father's approval, the other man must be regarded as the worthier.

Hermia   I wish my father saw things my way.

Theseus   Rather, you must see things as he does.

Hermia   I beg your Grace's pardon. I don't know what has given me the courage, nor whether it is proper for me to put my point of view forward here in such august company; but I beg your Grace to tell me what is the worst that can happen to me if I refuse to marry Demetrius?

Theseus   You must either suffer death, or have no further contact with men. Therefore, fair Hermia, think about what you want. Consider how young you are. Examine your feelings carefully. If you don't marry the man your father has chosen for you, could you tolerate wearing nun's clothes, and be cooped up forever in some shady cloister, a virgin all your life, singing quiet hymns to the cold and barren moon? Those who can control their passions and undertake a lifetime of virginity are blessed three times over, but here on earth the rose that gives off its perfume is happier than the one which, withering on the untouched stalk, grows, lives and dies in a state of single blessedness.

Hermia   So will I grow, so live, so die, my lord,
Ere I will yield my virgin patent up
Unto his lordship whose unwished yoke
My soul consents not to give sovereignty.

85 **Theseus**   Take time to pause, and by the next new moon,
The sealing-day betwixt my love and me
For everlasting bond of fellowship,
Upon that day either prepare to die
For disobedience to your father's will,
90   Or else to wed Demetrius, as he would,
Or on Diana's altar to protest
For aye, austerity and single life.

Demetrius   Relent, sweet Hermia, and Lysander, yield
Thy crazed title to my certain right.

95 **Lysander**   You have her father's love, Demetrius:
Let me have Hermia's; do you marry him.

Egeus   Scornful Lysander, true, he hath my love;
And what is mine my love shall render him;
And she is mine, and all my right of her
100   I do estate unto Demetrius.

Lysander   I am, my Lord, as well derived as he,
As well possessed; my love is more than his;
My fortunes every way as fairly ranked,
If not with vantage, as Demetrius';
105   And, which is more than all these boasts can be,
I am beloved of beauteous Hermia.
Why should not I then prosecute my right?
Demetrius, I'll avouch it to his head,
Made love to Nedar's daughter, Helena,
110   And won her soul: and she, sweet lady dotes,
Devoutly dotes, dotes in idolatry,
Upon this spotted and inconstant man.

Hermia So I will grow, and so live and so die, my lord,
rather than surrender my virginity to a husband whose
unwanted rule my soul could never agree to obey.

Theseus Take time to reconsider. By the next new moon,
my wedding day, either prepare to die for disobeying your
father's will, or else marry Demetrius as he wishes; or on
the altar of Diana, patroness of chastity, vow to live
forever a life of austerity, unmarried.

Demetrius Relent, sweet Hermia. Lysander, surrender your
flawed claim in deference to my undoubted right.

Lysander You have her father's love, Demetrius. Let me
have Hermia's. Marry him!

Egeus Yes, scornful Lysander, true, he has my love. And
because of that love I'll give to him what's mine. She
belongs to me, and I hand over all my rights in her to
Demetrius.

Lysander I am, my lord, of as good a family as he. I'm as
rich. I'm more in love than he is. In every way, my
prospects are equal to, if not better than, those of
Demetrius. And what's more important than all these
claims, Hermia loves me. Why, therefore, shouldn't I
press for my rights? I'll say it to his face: Demetrius
courted Helena – Nedar's daughter – and won her heart.
She, sweet lady, dotes on . . . worships . . . idolises . . .
this tainted and unfaithful man.

Theseus   I must confess that I have heard so much,
And with Demetrius thought to have spoke thereof:
115   But being over-full of self-affairs,
My mind did lose it. But Demetrius, come,
And come Egeus, you shall go with me;
I have some private schooling for you both.
For you, fair Hermia, look you arm yourself
120   To fit your fancies to your father's will;
Or else the law of Athens yields you up
(Which by no means we may extentuate)
To death, or to a vow of single life.
Come, my Hippolyta; what cheer, my love?
125   Demetrius and Egeus, go along:
I must employ you in some business
Against our nuptial, and confer with you
Of something nearly that concerns yourselves.

Egeus   With duty and desire we follow you.

[*Exeunt all but* **Lysander** *and* **Hermia**]

130 **Lysander**   How now, my love? Why is your cheek so pale?
How chance the roses there do fade so fast?

Hermia   Belike for want of rain, which I could well
Beteem them from the tempest of my eyes.

Lysander   Ay me! For aught that I could ever read,
135   Could ever hear by tale or history,
The course of true love never did run smooth;
But either it was different in blood –

Hermia   O cross! too high to be enthralled to low.

Lysander   Or else misgraffed, in respect of years –

140 **Hermia**   O spite! too old to be engaged to young.

Theseus   I must confess that I have heard as much, and I
was going to speak to Demetrius about it. Being
preoccupied with my own affairs, it slipped my mind.
Demetrius and Egeus: come with me. I've some advice
to give to you in private. As for you, fair Hermia: see that
your fancies fit in with your father's wishes, or else the
law of Athens, which I can't alter, condemns you to
death or lifelong chastity. [**Hippolyta** *looks dismayed*]
Come, my Hippolyta; take heart, my love. [*He makes to
go*] Demetrius and Egeus, come along. I must give you
some tasks in connection with our wedding celebrations,
and discuss your personal affairs.

Egeus   It's our duty and a pleasure to follow you.

[*They all leave except* **Lysander** *and* **Hermia**]

Lysander   Well then, my love: why these pale cheeks?
What's made the roses fade so fast?

Hermia   Probably lack of rain, which I could well provide
with storms of tears.

Lysander   Alas, judging by all I've ever read, or ever heard
of, in fact or fiction, 'the course of true love never did
run smooth'. It might be a class difference –

Hermia   Such a cross to bear! To be too high-born to fall
for a commoner!

Lysander   – or else the ages were ill-matched –

Hermia   How cruel! To be too old to marry someone young!

Lysander   Or else it stood upon the choice of friends –

Hermia   O hell! to choose love by another's eyes.

Lysander   Or, if there were a sympathy in choice,
War, death, or sickness did lay siege to it;
145 Making it momentary as a sound,
Swift as a shadow, short as any dream,
Brief as the lightning in the collied night,
That in a spleen unfolds both heaven and earth,
And ere a man hath power to say, 'Behold!',
150 The jaws of darkness do devour it up;
So quick bright things come to confusion.

Hermia   If then true lovers have been ever crossed,
It stands as an edict in destiny.
Then let us teach our trial patience,
155 Because it is a customary cross,
As due to love as thoughts, and dreams, and sighs,
Wishes and tears, poor fancy's followers.

Lysander   A good persuasion; therefore hear me, Hermia:
I have a widow aunt, a dowager
160 Of great revenue, and she hath no child;
From Athens is her house remote seven leagues,
And she respects me as her only son.
There, gentle Hermia, may I marry thee;
And to that place the sharp Athenian law
165 Cannot pursue us. If thou lov'st me, then,
Steal forth thy father's house tomorrow night;
And in the wood, a league without the town,
Where I did meet thee once with Helena
To do observance to a morn of May,
There will I stay for thee.

170 **Hermia**   My good Lysander,
I swear to thee by Cupid's strongest bow,

Lysander – or else relations had a say in it –

Hermia What hell! To have others make the choice . . . .

Lysander – or, even if the match pleased everyone, war, death or sickness menaced it. Then it's as temporary as a sound; as swift as a moving shadow; as short as a dream; as brief as lightning on a pitch-black night when it illuminates both heaven and earth in a fit of temper, and before you can say 'Look!' is swallowed again by darkness. That's how quickly bright hopes fade.

Hermia If true lovers always have been thwarted, then it must be a rule of life. So let's bear our suffering patiently, because it's a traditional cross to bear: as much a part of love as thoughts and dreams and sighs, wishes and tears, poor love's usual attendants.

Lysander Well said. So listen, Hermia. I have a widowed aunt, an elderly lady of great wealth, and she is childless. She regards me as her only son. Her house is about twenty miles from Athens, and there, gentle Hermia, I can marry you. The severe Athenian laws can't follow us there. If you love me, slip out of your father's house tomorrow night, and in the wood three miles outside the town, where I once met you with Helena one May morning, there I'll wait for you.

Hermia Good Lysander, I swear to you by Cupid's most powerful bow, by his best gold-tipped arrow, by the

By his best arrow with the golden head,
By the simplicity of Venus' doves,
By that which knitteth souls and prospers loves,
175 And by that fire which burned the Carthage Queen
When the false Troyan under sail was seen;
By all the vows that ever men have broke,
In number more than ever women spoke,
In that same place thou hast appointed me,
180 Tomorrow truly will I meet with thee.

Lysander   Keep promise, love. Look, here comes Helena.

[*Enter* **Helena**]

Hermia   God speed, fair Helena! Whither away?

Helena   Call you me fair? That fair again unsay!
Demetrius loves your fair. O happy fair!
185 Your eyes are lode-stars, and your tongue's sweet air
More tuneable than lark to shepherd's ear,
When wheat is green, when hawthorn buds appear.
Sickness is catching; O, were favour so,
Yours would I catch, fair Hermia, ere I go.
190 My ear should catch your voice, my eye your eye,
My tongue should catch your tongue's sweet melody.
Were all the world mine, Demetrius being bated,
The rest I'll give to be to you translated.
O teach me how you look and with what art
195 You sway the motion of Demetrius' heart!

Hermia   I frown upon him, yet he loves me still.

Helena   O that your frowns would teach my smiles such
skill!

Hermia   I give him curses, yet he gives me love.

200 **Helena**   O that my prayers could such affection move!

faithfulness of the sacred doves of Venus, by her magic girdle which unites souls and makes love flourish, by the fire in which Dido committed suicide on seeing the false Aeneas sail away, by all the vows that men have ever broken (many more than women have ever uttered!): I promise to meet you tomorrow at the appointed place.

Lysander   Keep your promise, my love. Look, here's Helena!

[**Helena** *enters, hurriedly*]

Hermia   [*pleasantly*] Safe journey fair Helena! Where are you going?

Helena   [*taking offence*] Who are you calling 'fair'? Take that 'fair' back! Demetrius loves your fairness: such fortunate beauty! To him, your eyes are magnetic, your speech is more pleasing than a lark's song to a shepherd in spring, when wheat is green and hawthorn buds appear. Sickness is infectious; I wish good looks were too. I'd catch yours, fair Hermia, before I left. My ear would catch your voice, my eye would catch your eye, my tongue would catch your tongue's sweet tunefulness. If I owned the world, I'd give it all, except Demetrius, to be turned into you. Teach me to look like you. Tell me how you attract Demetrius's love.

Hermia   I frown at him, yet he still loves me.

Helena   I wish your frowns could teach my smiles to do such clever tricks!

Hermia   I curse him, yet he loves me.

Helena   I wish my prayers could generate such affection!

Hermia   The more I hate, the more he follows me.

Helena   The more I love, the more he hateth me.

Hermia   His folly, Helena, is no fault of mine.

Helena   None but your beauty; would that fault were mine!

205 **Hermia**   Take comfort: he no more shall see my face;
Lysander and myself will fly this place.
Before the time I did Lysander see,
Seemed Athens as a paradise to me.
O then, what graces in my love do dwell,
210   That he hath turned a heaven unto a hell!

Lysander   Helen, to you our minds we will unfold.
Tomorrow night, when Phoebe doth behold
Her silver visage in the watery glass,
Decking with liquid pearl the bladed grass,
215   (A time that lovers' flights doth still conceal),
Through Athens' gates have we devised to steal.

Hermia   And in the wood, where often you and I
Upon faint primrose-beds were wont to lie,
Emptying our bosoms of their counsel sweet,
220   There, my Lysander and myself shall meet,
And thence from Athens turn away our eyes
To seek new friends and stranger companies.
Farewell, sweet playfellow; pray thou for us;
And good luck grant thee thy Demetrius.
225   Keep word, Lysander; we must starve our sight
From lovers' food, till morrow deep midnight.

[*Exit* **Hermia**]

Lysander   I will, my Hermia. Helena, adieu.
As you on him, Demetrius dote on you!

[*Exit* **Lysander**]

34

Hermia   The more I hate him, the more he follows me.

Helena   The more I love him, the more he hates me.

Hermia   His folly, Helena, is not my fault.

Helena   It's the fault of your beauty. I wish that fault was mine!

Hermia   Take comfort. He won't see my face again. Lysander and I are running away. Before I saw Lysander, Athens seemed like paradise. What qualities my loved one has, if he can turn a heaven into a hell!

Lysander   Helen, we'll confide in you. Tomorrow night, when the moon sees her reflection in the sea, and dew falls on the grass – just the right time for hiding elopements – we plan to steal through the gates of Athens.

Hermia   And in the wood, where you and I often used to lie on beds of pale primroses, confiding our secrets to each other, Lysander and I will meet. We'll turn our backs on Athens and seek new friends and the companionship of strangers. Farewell, sweet playfellow! Pray for us, and may good luck grant you your Demetrius. Keep your promise, Lysander; we must deny ourselves the joy of seeing each other till midnight tomorrow.

[*She goes*]

Lysander   I shall, my Hermia! Goodbye, Helena. Just as you dote on Demetrius, may he dote on you!

[**Lysander** *goes*]

Helena   How happy some o'er other some can be!
230   Through Athens I am thought as fair as she.
But what of that? Demetrius thinks not so;
He will not know what all but he do know:
And as he errs, doting on Hermia's eyes,
So I, admiring of his qualities.
235   Things base and vile, holding no quantity,
Love can transpose to form and dignity.
Love looks not with the eyes, but with the mind,
And therefore is winged Cupid painted blind.
Nor hath Love's mind of any judgement taste;
240   Wings, and no eyes, figure unheedy haste;
And therefore is Love said to be a child,
Because in choice he is so oft beguiled.
As waggish boys in game themselves forswear;
So the boy Love is perjured everywhere;
245   For ere Demetrius looked on Hermia's eyne,
He hailed down oaths that he was only mine;
And when this hail some heat from Hermia felt,
So he dissolved, and showers of oaths did melt.
I will go tell him of fair Hermia's flight;
250   Then to the wood will he tomorrow night
Pursue her; and for this intelligence,
If I have thanks, it is a dear expense.
But herein mean I to enrich my pain,
To have his sight thither, and back again.

[*Exit*]

Helena   How much happier some are than others. All
Athens thinks I'm as beautiful as she is. But what's the
use of that? Demetrius doesn't think so. He won't
accept what everyone else knows well: and just as he's
wrong to dote on Hermia's eyes, I'm at fault too for
admiring his qualities. Things that are base and vile, and
held in contempt, can be transformed by Love, and given
form and dignity. Love functions through the mind, not
sight: that's why winged Cupid is always depicted as
blind. Not that Love's mind has good judgement. Wings
and blindness suggest rash haste. Therefore Love is said
to be a child, because he's so often misled in making a
choice. Just as high-spirited boys trick each other in
sport, so the boy Love is deceived everywhere. Before
Demetrius took a fancy to Hermia, thick as hail he swore
his oaths to me alone. Then when the hail encountered
warmth from Hermia's direction, he broke faith, and his
showers of oaths all melted. I'll go and tell him of fair
Hermia's intention to run away. Then he'll follow her to
the wood tomorrow night. If he thanks me for the
information, he'll do it grudgingly. But this way I'll
indulge my suffering. We'll see each other again.

Scene 2

Athens. Enter **Quince** *the carpenter,* **Snug** *the joiner,*
Bottom *the weaver,* **Flute** *the bellows-mender,* **Snout** *the*
tinker, and **Starveling** *the tailor.*

Quince   Is all our company here?

Bottom   You were best to call them generally, man by
man, according to the scrip.

Quince   Here is the scroll of every man's name, which is
5   thought fit, through all Athens, to play in our interlude
before the Duke and the Duchess on his wedding-day at
night.

Bottom   First, good Peter Quince, say what the play treats
on: then read the names of the actors: and so grow to a
10   point.

Quince   Marry, our play is: 'The most lamentable comedy
and most cruel death of Pyramus and Thisbe'.

Bottom   A very good piece of work, I assure you, and a
merry. Now, good Peter Quince, call forth your actors by
15   the scroll. Masters, spread yourselves.

Quince   Answer as I call you. Nick Bottom, the weaver?

Bottom   Ready. Name what part I am for, and proceed.

Quince   You, Nick Bottom, are set down for Pyramus.

Bottom   What is Pyramus? A lover or a tyrant?

20 **Quince**   A lover, that kills himself most gallant for love.

Bottom   That will ask some tears in the true performing of
it. If I do it, let the audience look to their eyes: I will move

Scene 2

Enter **Quince** *the carpenter, carrying a bundle of papers,*
Snug *the joiner,* **Bottom** *the weaver,* **Flute** *the bellows-*
mender, **Snout** *the tinker, and* **Starveling** *the tailor.*

Quince   Is everyone here?

Bottom   You'd better call them overall – man by
man – according to the script. [*He points to* **Quince's**
documents]

Quince   Here's the list of names of all the men in Athens
thought fit to take part in our play, which is to
be performed before the Duke and the Duchess on his
wedding day, at night.

Bottom   First, good Peter Quince, say what the play's
about. Then read the names of the actors, and so come
to a full stop.

Quince   Well, our play's called 'The most distressing
comedy, and most cruel death, of Pyramus and Thisbe'.

Bottom   A very good piece of work, I assure you, and very
entertaining. Now, good Peter Quince, call your actors
from the list. Gentlemen, spread yourselves out.

Quince   Answer as I call you. Nick Bottom, the weaver?

Bottom   Ready, Tell me my part, and proceed.

Quince   You, Nick Bottom, have been given Pyramus.

Bottom   Who's Pyramus? A lover, or a mighty hero?

Quince   A lover, who kills himself very gallantly for love.

Bottom   That'll require some tears to do it well. If I do it,
let the audience take care of their eyes. I'll rant my

39

storms; I will condole in some measure. To the rest – yet
my chief humour is for a tyrant. I could play Ercles
25 rarely, or a part to tear a cat in, to make all split:

> The raging rocks,
> And shivering shocks,
> Shall break the locks
>   Of prison-gates;
30 And Phibbus' car
> Shall shine from far
> And make and mar
>   The foolish fates.

This was lofty! Now name the rest of the players. This is
35 Ercles' vein, a tyrant's vein: a lover is more condoling.

Quince   Francis Flute, the bellows-mender?

Flute   Here, Peter Quince.

Quince   Flute, you must take Thisbe on you.

Flute   What is Thisbe? A wandering knight?

40 **Quince**   It is the lady that Pyramus must love.

Flute   Nay, faith, let not me play a woman; I have a beard
coming.

Quince   That's all one; you shall play it in a mask, and you
may speak as small as you will.

45 **Bottom**   An I may hide my face, let me play Thisbe too.
I'll speak in a monstrous little voice: 'Thisne, Thisne'. 'Ah
Pyramus, my lover dear! thy Thisbe dear, and lady dear!'

passion and rave my grief. And all that sort of thing. But my real gift is for playing heroic parts. I could be a great Hercules, or play a swaggerer, well enough to raise the roof. [*He gives a demonstration*]

> The raging rocks,
> And shivering shocks
> Shall break the locks
>   Of prison-gates.
> The sun, bright star,
> Shall shine from far
> And make and mar
>   The foolish fates.

Lofty stuff! Now name the rest of the players. [*Explaining*] That's the Hercules style: the heroic style. A lover is more tear-jerking.

Quince   [*reading from his list*] Francis Flute, the bellows-mender?

Flute   [*His voice is high-pitched*] Here, Peter Quince.

Quince   Flute, you must take on Thisbe.

Flute   Who's Thisbe? A wandering knight?

Quince   It's the lady Pyramus will love.

Flute   No, really; don't let me play a woman. I've got a beard coming.

Quince   That doesn't matter. You can play it in a mask. And you can speak in as tiny a voice as you wish.

Bottom   If I can hide my face, let me play Thisbe too. I'll speak in an extraordinary little voice. [*First his Pyramus voice*] 'Thisne, Thisne!' [*Changing to a falsetto*] 'Ah, Pyramus, my lover dear! Your Thisbe dear, and lady dear!'

Quince   No, no, you must play Pyramus; and Flute, you
Thisbe.

50 **Bottom**   Well, proceed.

Quince   Robin Starveling, the tailor?

Starveling   Here, Peter Quince.

Quince   Robin Starveling, you must play Thisbe's mother.
Tom Snout, the tinker?

55 **Snout**   Here, Peter Quince.

Quince   You, Pyramus' father; myself, Thisbe's father; Snug
the joiner, you, the lion's part: and I hope, here is a play
fitted.

Snug   Have you the lion's part written? Pray you, if it be,
60   give it me, for I am slow of study.

Quince   You may do it extempore, for it is nothing but
roaring.

Bottom   Let me play the lion too; I will roar that I will do
any man's heart good to hear me. I will roar, that I will
65   make the Duke say, 'Let him roar again, let him roar
again!'

Quince   And you should do it too terribly, you would fright
the Duchess and the ladies, and they would shriek; and
that were enough to hang us all.

70 **All**   That would hang us, every mother's son.

Bottom   I grant you, friends, if you should fright the ladies
out of their wits, they would have no more discretion but
to hang us; but I will aggravate my voice so, that I will
roar you as gently as any sucking dove; I will roar you an't
75   were any nightingale.

Quince No, no. You must play Pyramus. And Flute – you Thisbe.

Bottom Well. Proceed.

Quince Robin Starveling, the tailor?

Starveling Here, Peter Quince.

Quince Robin Starveling, you must play Thisbe's mother. Tom Snout, the tinker?

Snout Here, Peter Quince.

Quince You, Pyramus's father. Myself – Thisbe's father. Snug the joiner – you the part of the lion. I hope that sorts out the cast.

Snug Have you got the lion's lines written out? If so, please give them to me – I'm very slow at learning.

Quince You can make it up. It's nothing but roaring.

Bottom Let me play the lion, too! I'll roar so it will do any man's heart a power of good to hear me. I'll roar so that the Duke will say 'Make him roar again. Make him roar again!'

Quince If you did it too terrifyingly, you'd frighten the Duchess and the ladies, and make them scream. That would be enough to have us all hanged.

All [*nodding solemnly*] We'd all be hanged, every mother's son.

Bottom I grant you, friends, that if you frightened the ladies out of their wits, they'd hang us for sure. But I'll so aggravate my voice that I'll roar for you as gently as any sucking dove. I'll roar for you like a nightingale.

Quince   You can play no part but Pyramus; for Pyramus is a sweet-faced man, a proper man as one shall see in a summer's day, a most lovely, gentleman-like man; therefore you must needs play Pyramus.

80 **Bottom**   Well, I will undertake it. What beard were I best to play it in?

Quince   Why, what you will.

Bottom   I will discharge it in either your straw-colour beard, your orange-tawny beard, your purple-in-grain
85   beard, or your French-crown-colour beard, your perfect yellow.

Quince   Some of your French crowns have no hair at all, and then you will play bare-faced. But, masters, here are your parts, and I am to entreat you, request you, and
90   desire you, to con them by tomorrow night; and meet me in the palace wood, a mile without the town, by moonlight. There will we rehearse: for if we meet in the city, we shall be dogged with company, and our devices known. In the mean time I will draw a bill of properties,
95   such as our play wants. I pray you, fail me not.

Bottom   We will meet, and there we may rehearse most obscenely and courageously. Take pains; be perfect; adieu!

Quince   At the Duke's oak we meet.

Bottom   Enough; hold or cut bow-strings.

[*Exeunt*]

Quince You can only play Pyramus. Pyramus is a nice-looking man; as fine a man as you'll see on a summer's day. A really lovely, gentlemanly man. Therefore you must play Pyramus.

Bottom Well, I'll take it on. What's the best beard for me to play it in?

Quince Whichever you like.

Bottom I'll perform it in either a straw-coloured beard, a tan-coloured beard, a fast-dyed red beard, or a perfect yellow beard like a French gold crown.

Quince Some French crowns have lost all their hair – so you'd have to play it clean-shaven! [*The men enjoy the joke hugely*] But, gentlemen, here are your parts. [*He passes them round*] I must entreat you, request you and require you to learn them by tomorrow night, and to meet me in the palace wood, a mile outside the town, by moonlight. We'll rehearse there. If we meet in the city, we'll have onlookers and our production will become known to the public. In the meantime, I'll draw up a list of the props our play needs. Now don't let me down.

Bottom We'll meet, and we'll be able to rehearse there most obscenely and courageously. Make an effort. Be word-perfect. Adieu!

Quince We'll meet at the Duke's oak tree.

Bottom Right. [*To the men*] Be there – or beware!

[*They go*]

Act two

Scene 1

A wood near Athens. Enter a **Fairy** *at one side, and* **Puck** *at another.*

Puck How now, spirit, whither wander you?

Fairy Over hill over dale,
　　Thorough bush, thorough briar,
　Over park over pale,
5　　Thorough flood, thorough fire,
　I do wander everywhere,
　Swifter than the moon's sphere;
　　And I serve the fairy queen,
　　To dew her orbs upon the green.
10　　The cowslips tall her pensioners be,
　　In their gold coats spots you see;
　　Those be rubies, fairy favours,
　　In those freckles live their savours.
　I must go seek some dew-drops here,
15　And hang a pearl in every cowslip's ear.

　Farewell, thou lob of spirits; I'll be gone;
　Our queen and all her elves come here anon.

　Puck The king doth keep his revels here tonight;
　Take heed the queen come not within his sight;
20　For Oberon is passing fell and wrath,
　Because that she as her attendant hath
　A lovely boy stolen from an Indian king;
　She never had so sweet a changeling.
　And jealous Oberon would have the child

Act two

Scene 1

A wood. Enter a **Fairy** *from one side and* **Puck** *from the other.*

Puck   Greetings, spirit! Where are you going?

Fairy   Over hill, over dale,
    Through bush, through briar,
  Over park, over fence,
    Through flood, through fire.
  I wander over every place
  Swifter than the moon through space.
    I'm servant of the fairy queen's –
    I dew the rings on village greens.
    Her bodyguards are cowslips tall:
    Their coats are golden, spotted all
    With rubies, which are fairy presents:
    In those freckles live their sweet scents.
  I must seek out some dew-drops here
  And hang a pearl in every cowslip's ear.

  Farewell, you tom-fool sprite; I'll disappear.
  Our queen, with all her elves, will soon be here.

Puck   The king is celebrating here tonight;
  Make sure the queen comes not within his sight –
  For Oberon is in a furious rage
  Because she's taken as her private page
  A lovely boy, stolen from an Indian king:
  She never had so sweet a plaything.
  And jealous Oberon would wish the child

25   Knight of his train, to trace the forests wild;
     But she perforce withholds the loved boy,
     Crowns him with flowers, and makes him all her joy.
     And now they never meet in grove or green,
     By fountain clear, or spangled starlight sheen,
30   But they do square, that all their elves for fear
     Creep into acorn cups and hide them there.

Fairy   Either I mistake your shape and making quite,
     Or else you are that shrewd and knavish sprite
     Called Robin Goodfellow. Are not you he,
35   That frights the maidens of the villagery,
     Skim milk, and sometimes labour in the quern,
     And bootless make the breathless housewife churn,
     And sometimes make the drink to bear no barm,
     Mislead night-wanderers, laughing at their harm?
40   Those that Hobgoblin call you, and sweet Puck,
     You do their work, and they shall have good luck.
     Are not you he?

Puck   Thou speak'st aright;
     I am that merry wanderer of the night.
     I jest to Oberon, and make him smile,
45   When I a fat and bean-fed horse beguile,
     Neighing in likeness of a filly foal;
     And sometimes lurk I in a gossip's bowl,
     In very likeness of a roasted crab;
     And when she drinks, against her lips I bob,
50   And on her withered dewlap pour the ale.
     The wisest aunt, telling the saddest tale,
     Sometime for three-foot stool mistaketh me;
     Then slip I from her bum, down topples she,
     And 'tailor' cries, and falls into a cough;
55   And then the whole quire hold their hips, and laugh,
     And waxen in their mirth, and neeze and swear
     A merrier hour was never wasted there.
     But room, fairy! Here comes Oberon.

To be his follower through the forests wild;
But she, by force, witholds the favoured boy –
Crowns him with flowers, and makes him all her joy.
So now they never meet in grove or green,
By fountains clear, or where the stars are seen,
Without a quarrel starting. All their elves, from fright,
Creep into acorn cups, out of their sight.

Fairy   Either I'm mistaken by your features
Or you're that most mischievous of creatures
Called Robin Goodfellow. Have you not made
The maidens of the village all afraid?
Skimmed the milk? Meddled at the butter-press?
Made the breathless housewife churn without success?
Stopped the brew from turning into beer?
Misled night-travellers, laughing at their fear?
'Hobgoblin' they all call you, and 'Sweet Puck'.
You do their work, and that is their good luck!
Aren't you he?

Puck   You've got it right.
I am that merry wanderer of the night.
I'm Oberon's jester. I make him laugh.
I trick a fat horse (fed on beans, not chaff)
by neighing to sound like a female foal.
Sometimes I hide in an old gossip's bowl –
I'm the apple that's used to heat the beer.
When she drinks, against her lips I appear
And down her sagging chins I pour the ale.
The wise old crone as she tells her sad tale,
Mistakes me sometimes for a three-legged stool.
I slip from her bum; she topples, the fool,
Crying 'My poor arse!' Then she starts to cough
Which makes them all laugh, and starts them all off!
Their mirth knows no bounds; they sneeze as they say
They've never laughed more than on that jolly day.
But stand aside, fairy! Here comes Oberon!

49

Fairy   And here my mistress! Would that he were gone!

[*Enter* **Oberon** *the king of fairies at one side with his train,
and* **Titania** *the queen at another with hers*]

60 **Oberon**   Ill met by moonlight, proud Titania.

Titania   What, jealous Oberon? Fairies, skip hence:
I have forsworn his bed and company.

Oberon   Tarry, rash wanton; am not I thy lord?

Titania   Then I must be thy lady; but I know
65 When thou hast stolen away from fairy land,
And in the shape of Corin sat all day,
Playing on pipes of corn, and versing love
To amorous Phillida. Why art thou here,
Come from the farthest step of India,
70 But that, forsooth, the bouncing Amazon,
Your buskined mistress, and your warrior love,
To Theseus must be wedded; and you come
To give their bed joy and prosperity.

Oberon   How canst thou thus, for shame, Titania,
75 Glance at my credit with Hippolyta,
Knowing I know thy love to Theseus?
Didst thou not lead him through the glimmering night
From Perigouna, whom he ravished?
And make him with fair Aegles break his faith,
80 With Ariadne, and Antiopa?

Titania   These are the forgeries of jealousy;
And never since the middle summer's spring
Met we on hill, in dale, forest, or mead,
By paved fountain, or by rushy brook,
85 Or in the beached margent of the sea,
To dance our ringlets to the whistling wind,
But with thy brawls thou hast disturbed our sport.

Fairy   And here comes my lady – if only Oberon would go!

[*Enter* **Oberon**, *king of the fairies, with his attendants.
From the opposite direction,* **Titania** *the queen enters
with hers*]

Oberon   How unfortunate to meet you here in the
moonlight, proud Titania!

Titania   [*recognising him she halts abruptly*] What? Jealous
Oberon? Fairies, let's go. I've vowed to turn my back on
him.

Oberon   Not so fast, madam! Am I not your husband?

Titania   Then I must be your wife – but I've known you to
slip away from fairyland and take human shape as the
shepherd Corin, sitting all day long playing on your pipes
and writing love-poems to eager Phyllis. What has
brought you here from the farthest corner of India, if it
isn't – let's face it! – that the ravishing queen of the
Amazons, your heart-throb in hunting-boots, your warrior
lady-love, is to wed Theseus, and you want to bestow
joy and prosperity on their marriage?

Oberon   For shame, Titania! How can you make snide
remarks about Hippolyta, when you know I'm well aware
of your fondness for Theseus? Didn't you conduct him
safely through the shades of night after he had raped
Perigouna? And didn't you make him jilt Aegles, and
desert Ariadne and Antiopa?

Titania   These are the fantasies of jealousy! Since early
June, never have we met to dance our fairy rings to the
music of the winds – whether on hills, in valleys, forests
or meadows, by pebble- bottomed fountains or rush-
strewn brooks, or on sandy beaches – without you
ruining our enjoyment by your misbehaviour. So much so,

Therefore the winds, piping to us in vain,
As in revenge have sucked up from the sea
90 Contagious fogs; which, falling in the land,
Have every pelting river made so proud
That they have overborne their continents.
The ox hath therefore stretched his yoke in vain,
The ploughman lost his sweat, and the green corn
95 Hath rotted ere his youth attained a beard:
The fold stands empty in the drowned field,
And crows are fatted with the murrion flock;
The nine-men's-morris is filled up with mud,
And the quaint mazes in the wanton green,
100 For lack of tread, are undistinguishable.
The human mortals want their winter cheer;
No night is now with hymn or carol blest;
Therefore the moon, the governess of floods,
Pale in her anger, washes all the air,
105 That rheumatic diseases do abound.
And thorough this distemperature we see
The seasons alter: hoary-headed frosts
Fall in the fresh lap of the crimson rose,
And on old Hiems' thin and icy crown
110 An odorous chaplet of sweet summer buds
Is, as in mockery, set. The spring, the summer,
The childing autumn, angry winter, change
Their wonted liveries, and the mazed world,
By their increase, now knows not which is which.
115 And this same progeny of evils comes
From our debate, from our dissension;
We are their parents and original.

Oberon   Do you amend it, then; it lies in you.
Why should Titania cross her Oberon?
120 I do but beg a little changeling boy
To be my henchman.

that the winds, playing for us in vain, have taken revenge
by sucking up unhealthy mists from the sea. These,
turning to rain over the land, have swollen all the little
rivers till they've burst their banks. Oxen have pulled
the plough in vain. Ploughmen have wasted their
labour. Unripe corn has rotted before it could mature.
Sheepfolds stand empty in the flooded fields. Crows
gorge themselves on the corpses of the plague-ridden
sheep. Mud obliterates the sites of outdoor games such
as 'nine men's morris'. Meandering cross-country paths
are unrecognisable in the overgrown fields, through lack
of use. Human beings are denied their winter pleasures:
no hymns or sing-songs brighten their evenings. Therefore the moon, controller of the tides, quite pale with
anger, causes rainstorms, resulting in diseases caused by
dampness. Because of this inclement weather, we see
the seasons alter. Heavy frosts fall just as crimson roses
bloom. A chain of sweet and perfumed summer buds is,
as if in mockery, set in the thin ice of long-lived Winter.
Spring, summer, fruitful autumn, and angry winter
exchange their usual features. The bewildered world
can't tell one from the other by their produce. And all
these offsprings of evil come from our quarrel, from our
disagreement. We are their parents; we originated them.

Oberon Put it right, then. It's up to you. Why should
Titania go against her Oberon's wishes? I'm only asking
for a little changeling boy, to be my page.

Titania   Set your heart at rest;
          The fairy land buys not the child of me.
          His mother was a votaress of my order,
          And in the spiced Indian air, by night,
125   Full often hath she gossiped by my side;
          And sat with me on Neptune's yellow sands,
          Marking the embarked traders on the flood;
          When we have laughed to see the sails conceive,
          And grow big-bellied with the wanton wind;
130   Which she with pretty and with swimming gait
          Following, her womb then rich with my young squire,
          Would imitate, and sail upon the land
          To fetch me trifles, and return again,
          As from a voyage, rich with merchandise.
135   But she, being mortal, of that boy did die;
          And for her sake do I rear up her boy,
          And for her sake I will not part with him.

Oberon   How long within this wood intend you stay?

Titania   Perchance till after Theseus' wedding-day.
140   If you will patiently dance in our round,
          And see our moonlight revels, go with us;
          If not, shun me, and I will spare your haunts.

Oberon   Give me that boy, and I will go with thee.

Titania   Not for thy fairy kingdom. Fairies, away!
145   We shall chide downright, if I longer stay.

                              [*Exit* **Titania** *and her train*]

Oberon   Well, go thy way; thou shalt not from this grove,
          Till I torment thee for this injury.
          My gentle Puck, come hither. Thou rememb'rest
          Since once I sat upon a promontory,
150   And heard a mermaid on a dolphin's back

Titania Put your mind at rest. I wouldn't sell my child for all fairyland. His mother was a dedicated follower of mine, and in the scented evening air of India she's often gossiped by my side, and sat with me on beaches, watching departing cargo ships out at sea. We've laughed to see the sails billow and swell in the playful wind. And being pregnant herself with my young attendant, she'd copy them on land, gliding along in a charming manner as if through water to fetch me this and that. Back she'd come like a ship from a voyage, loaded with merchandise. But being a mere mortal, she died in childbirth, and for her sake I'm bringing up her boy. And for her sake, I won't part with him.

Oberon How long do you intend to stay here in this wood?

Titania Perhaps till after Theseus's wedding day. If you'll be reasonable and dance with us in our fairy ring, and watch our moonlight merrymaking, come with us. If not, keep away from me, and I'll give your territory a wide berth.

Oberon Give me that boy, and I'll come with you.

Titania Not for your fairy kingdom! Fairies, let's away. We'll have a blazing row if I stay any longer.

[**Titania** *leaves with her attendants*]

Oberon Well go then. You won't leave this grove till I've made you suffer for this insult! Gentle Puck, come here. Do you remember the time when I sat on a jutting rock and heard a mermaid on a dolphin's back singing with

Uttering such dulcet and harmonious breath
That the rude sea grew civil at her song,
And certain stars shot madly from their spheres
To hear the sea-maid's music?

Puck   I remember.

155 **Oberon**   That very time I saw, but thou couldst not,
Flying between the cold moon and the earth,
Cupid all armed; a certain aim he took
At a fair vestal throned by the west
And loosed his love-shaft smartly from his bow
160 As it should pierce a hundred thousand hearts;
But I might see young Cupid's fiery shaft
Quenched in the chaste beams of the watery moon;
And the imperial votaress passed on,
In maiden meditation, fancy-free.
165 Yet marked I where the bolt of Cupid fell:
It fell upon a little western flower;
Before, milk-white, now purple with love's wound,
And maidens call it 'Love-in-idleness'.
Fetch me that flower, the herb I shewed thee once.
170 The juice of it on sleeping eyelids laid
Will make or man or woman madly dote
Upon the next live creature that it sees.
Fetch me this herb, and be thou here again
Ere the leviathan can swim a league.

175 **Puck**   I'll put a girdle round about the earth
In forty minutes.

[*Exit* **Puck**]

Oberon   Having once this juice,
I'll watch Titania when she is asleep,

such sweetness and harmony that the rough sea grew calm and certain stars shot madly out of their orbits on hearing the mermaid's music?

Puck   I remember.

Oberon   That selfsame time I saw armed Cupid, (though you could not) flying between the cold moon and the earth. He took true aim at a chaste queen ruling a western island. He fired an arrow of love smartly from his bow with enough force to pierce a hundred thousand hearts. The pure beams of the pale moon stopped young Cupid's passionate arrow. So the royal virgin passed on, thinking her maidenly thoughts, unconcerned with love. But I took note of where Cupid's arrow fell. It fell upon a little western flower; white originally, now purple with love's wound. Maidens call it 'love-in-idleness': the pansy. Fetch me that flower; I showed it to you once. If its juice is laid on sleeping eye-lids, the man or woman is made to fall madly in love with the next creature they see. Fetch me this flower, and come back again before a giant whale can swim three miles.

Puck   I'll encircle the earth in forty minutes!

[*He goes*]

Oberon   Once I've got this juice, I'll watch Titania when she's asleep, and put a droplet in her eyes. Then the next

And drop the liquor of it in her eyes:
The next thing then she waking looks upon,
180 Be it on lion, bear, or wolf, or bull,
On meddling monkey, or on busy ape,
She shall pursue it with the soul of love.
And ere I take this charm from off her sight,
As I can take it with another herb,
185 I'll make her render up her page to me.
But who comes here? I am invisible,
And I will overhear their conference.

[*Enter* **Demetrius**, **Helena** *following him*]

Demetrius   I love thee not, therefore pursue me not.
Where is Lysander, and fair Hermia?
190 The one I'll slay, the other slayeth me.
Thou told'st me they were stolen unto this wood;
And here am I, and wood within this wood,
Because I cannot meet my Hermia.
Hence, get thee gone, and follow me no more!

195 **Helena**   You draw me, you hard-hearted adamant,
But yet you draw not iron, for my heart
Is true as steel. Leave you your power to draw,
And I shall have no power to follow you.

Demetrius   Do I entice you? Do I speak you fair?
200 Or rather do I not in plainest truth
Tell you I do not nor I cannot love you?

Helena   And even for that do I love you the more.
I am your spaniel; and, Demetrius,
The more you beat me, I will fawn on you.
205 Use me but as your spaniel; spurn me, strike me,
Neglect me, lose me; only give me leave,
Unworthy as I am, to follow you.

thing she sees when she awakes – whether it's a lion, a bear, a wolf, or a bull, a mischievous monkey, or an active ape – she'll follow it madly in love. And before I remove the spell from her sight, which I can do with another herb, I'll make her give up her page to me. But who comes here? [*He makes a motion with his hand*] I am invisible, and I'll overhear their conversation.

[**Demetrius** *enters, followed by* **Helena**]

Demetrius   I don't love you, so stop following me! Where are Lysander and the beautiful Hermia? I'll kill Lysander; Hermia is killing me. You told me they'd hidden in this wood. Here I am, out of my mind within this wood because I cannot find my Hermia. Be off with you! Stop following me!

Helena   You attract me, you hard-hearted magnet. Not that I'm iron; my heart is true as steel. Lose your magnetism; then I won't be able to follow you.

Demetrius   Do I encourage you? Do I speak nicely to you? On the contrary – don't I tell you bluntly that I do not love you and never could?

Helena   I love you all the more for saying that. I'm your spaniel. Spurn me. Strike me. Neglect me. Lose me. Just allow me, unworthy as I am, to follow you. What

What worser place can I beg in your love,
And yet a place of high respect with me,
210   Than to be used as you do use your dog?

Demetrius   Tempt not too much the hatred of my spirit;
For I am sick when I do look on thee.

Helena   And I am sick when I look not on you.

Demetrius   You do impeach your modesty too much,
215   To leave the city and commit yourself
Into the hands of one that loves you not;
To trust the opportunity of night
And the ill counsel of a desert place
With the rich worth of your virginity.

220 **Helena**   Your virtue is my privilege: for that
It is not night when I do see your face,
Therefore I think I am not in the night;
Nor doth this wood lack worlds of company,
For you, in my respect, are all the world.
225   Then how can it be said I am alone,
When all the world is here to look on me?

Demetrius   I'll run from thee and hide me in the brakes,
And leave thee to the mercy of wild beasts.

Helena   The wildest hath not such a heart as you.
230   Run when you will, the story shall be changed:
Apollo flies, and Daphne holds the chase;
The dove pursues the griffin, the mild hind
Makes speed to catch the tiger; bootless speed,
When cowardice pursues, and valour flies!

235 **Demetrius**   I will not stay thy questions; let me go;
Or, if thou follow me, do not believe
But I shall do thee mischief in the wood.

humbler place can I beg in your love – though to me it's a place of pride – than to be treated as you would your dog?

Demetrius   Don't push me too hard. It makes me sick to look at you.

Helena   And I am sick when I'm *not* looking at you.

Demetrius   You put your reputation too much at risk: to leave the city, to put yourself at the mercy of someone who doesn't love you, and to expose your virginity to the hazards of night-time and the evil thoughts that lonely places generate.

Helena   Your virtue is my safeguard, because when I see your face, it isn't night – therefore I don't think I'm out at night. Nor is this wood short of ample company, for in my eyes, you are all the world, so how can it be said that I'm alone, when all the world is here to look at me?

Demetrius   I'll run away from you, and hide myself in the bushes, and leave you to the mercy of the wild beasts!

Helena   The wildest hasn't got a heart like yours! Run if you must. We'll reverse the old story. We'll have Apollo running away, and Daphne doing the chasing; the dove pursuing the griffin; the timid deer chasing the tiger! Pointless flight, when the coward does the pursuing, and the brave one runs off!

Demetrius   I won't bandy words with you here. Let me go! Or, if you follow me, don't doubt I'll do you some mischief in the wood.

Helena   Ay, in the temple, in the town, the field
     You do me mischief. Fie, Demetrius!
240   Your wrongs do set a scandal on my sex:
     We cannot fight for love, as men may do;
     We should be wooed, and were not made to woo.

                      [*Exit* **Demetrius**]

     I'll follow thee, and make a heaven of hell,
     To die upon the hand I love so well.

                            [*Exit*]

245 **Oberon**   Fare thee well, nymph: ere he do leave this grove,
     Thou shalt fly him, and he shall seek thy love.

     [*Enter* **Puck**]

     Hast thou the flower there? Welcome, wanderer.

Puck   Ay, there it is.

Oberon   I pray thee give it me.
     I know a bank whereon the wild thyme blows;
250   Where oxlips and the nodding violet grows,
     Quite over-canopied with luscious woodbine,
     With sweet musk-roses, and with eglantine;
     There sleeps Titania sometime of the night,
     Lulled in those flowers with dances and delight;
255   And there the snake throws her enamelled skin,
     Weed wide enough to wrap a fairy in;
     And with the juice of this I'll streak her eyes,
     And make her full of hateful fantasies.
     Take thou some of it, and seek through this grove:
260   A sweet Athenian lady is in love
     With a disdainful youth: anoint his eyes;

Helena   Yes, you do me mischief whether I'm in church, in town, or in the country. Really, Demetrius, your offensiveness brings disgrace upon my sex. We can't fight for love, as men can. We should be wooed: we weren't made to woo!

[**Demetrius** *runs off*]

I'll follow you, and find happiness in my misery − I'll die by the hand I love so well!

[**Helena** *follows him*]

Oberon   Farewell, young lady. Before he leaves this grove, you'll be running away from him. He'll be seeking *your* love.

[**Puck** *returns*]

Have you got the flower there? Welcome, wanderer.

Puck   Yes, there it is.

Oberon   Give it to me, please. I know a bank on which wild thyme blows in the wind; where oxlips grow, and violets nod their heads. Over it, there's a canopy of dense honeysuckle, with sweet-smelling ramblers and wild roses interspersed. Sometimes Titania sleeps there at night, lulled to sleep amongst the flowers after dancing and merrymaking. There, snakes shed their brightly-coloured skins, which are large enough for fairies to wrap themselves in. And with the juice of this [**Oberon** *holds the pansy aloft*] I'll smear her eyes, and put indelicate notions in her mind. [*To* **Puck**] You take some of it, and go searching through this grove. A sweet Athenian lady is in love with a youth who rejects her. Anoint his eyes,

But do it when the next thing he espies
May be the lady. Thou shalt know the man
By the Athenian garments he hath on.
265   Effect it with some care, that he may prove
More fond on her than she upon her love;
And look thou meet me ere the first cock crow.

Puck   Fear not, my lord; your servant shall do so.

[*Exeunt*]

Scene 2

The wood. Enter **Titania** *with her train.*

Titania   Come now, a roundel, and a fairy song;
5   Then, for the third part of a minute, hence;
Some to kill cankers in the musk-rose buds,
Some war with rere-mice for their leathern wings,
To make my small elves coats, and some keep back
The clamorous owl that nightly hoots and wonders
10   At our quaint spirits. Sing me now asleep;
Then to your offices, and let me rest.

[*The* **Fairies** *sing*]

1st Fairy   *You spotted snakes with double tongue,*
Thorny hedgehogs, be not seen;
Newts and blind-worms, do no wrong,
15   *Come not near our fairy queen.*

but do it when the next thing he sees will be the lady.
You'll know the man by the Athenian clothes he is
wearing. Do it carefully, so he'll be more infatuated with
her than she with him. See you meet me again before
morning breaks.

Puck   Don't worry, my lord. You servant will obey.

[*They go*]

Scene 2

Titania's *sleeping-place in the wood.* **Titania** *is with her fairy
followers.*

Titania   Come now: let's dance in a ring and sing a fairy
song! Then, for twenty seconds, depart: some to kill
caterpillars in the rosebuds; some to hunt bats for their
leather wings, to make coats for my small elves; and
some to hold off the noisy owl that hoots every night in
surprise at our daintiness. Sing me to sleep now, then go
to your duties and let me rest.

1st Fairy   [*singing*]

*You spotted snakes with two-pronged tongues
And spikey hedgehogs – don't be seen!
Newts and slow-worms – do no wrong!
Don't come near our fairy queen.*

65

Chorus   *Philomel, with melody,*
               Sing in our sweet lullaby;
               Lulla, lulla, lullaby; lulla, lulla, lullaby;
               Never harm, nor spell, nor charm,
20   *Come our lovely lady nigh;*
               So goodnight, with lullaby.

2nd Fairy   *Weaving spiders, come not here,*
               Hence, you long-legged spinners, hence!
               Beetles black, approach not near;
25   *Worm nor snail, do no offence.*

Chorus   *Philomel with melody, etc.*

[**Titania** *sleeps*]

1st Fairy   Hence away! Now all is well;
               One aloof stand sentinel.

[*Exeunt* **Fairies**]

[*Enter* **Oberon**, *who squeezes the juice on* **Titania's** *eyelids*]

Oberon   What thou seest when thou dost wake,
30   Do it for thy true love take;
               Love and languish for his sake.
               Be it ounce, or cat, or bear,
               Pard, or boar with bristled hair,
               In thy eye that shall appear
35   When thou waks't, it is thy dear.
               Wake when some vile thing is near.

[*Exit*]

[*Enter* **Lysander** *and* **Hermia**]

Chorus of fairies *Nightingale, with melody*
  Sing in our sweet lullaby:
  Lulla, lulla, lullaby; lulla, lulla, lullaby.

  No harm, nor spell, nor charm,
  Come our lovely lady nigh;
  So goodnight, with lullaby.

2nd Fairy *Weaving spiders, don't come here!*
  Away, you long-legged spinners! Hence!
  Black beetles, don't come near!
  Worms and snails – give no offence!

Chorus *Nightingale, with melody, etc.*

[**Titania** *falls asleep*]

1st Fairy Let's go. Now all is well. One of you stand on
  guard.

[*All the* **Fairies** *but one depart;* **Oberon** *enters, still invisible*]

Oberon [*squeezing the juice on* **Titania's** *eyelids*]

  What you see when you awake,
  Fall in love with, by mistake!
  Love and suffer for his sake!
  Be it lynx, wild cat, or bear;
  Leopard, boar with bristly hair –
  Whatever to your eyes appears
  When you awake, its sight endears.
  Wake when something nasty nears!

[*He goes*]

[**Lysander** *and* **Hermia** *enter*]

Lysander   Fair love, you faint with wandering in the wood,
And to speak truth, I have forgot our way.
We'll rest us, Hermia, if you think it good,
40   And tarry for the comfort of the day.

Hermia   Be it so, Lysander; find you out a bed,
For I upon this bank will rest my head.

Lysander   One turf shall serve as pillow for us both;
One heart, one bed, two bosoms, and one troth.

45 **Hermia**   Nay, good Lysander; for my sake, my dear,
Lie further off yet, do not lie so near.

Lysander   O take the sense, sweet, of my innocence!
Love takes the meaning in love's conference.
I mean that my heart unto yours is knit,
50   So that but one heart we can make of it.
Two bosoms interchained with an oath,
So then, two bosoms, and a single troth.
Then by your side no bed-room me deny,
For lying so, Hermia, I do not lie.

55 **Hermia**   Lysander riddles very prettily;
Now much beshrew my manners and my pride,
If Hermia meant to say Lysander lied!
But, gentle friend, for love and courtesy
Lie further off, in human modesty;
60   Such separation as may well be said
Becomes a virtuous bachelor and a maid;
So far be distant, and good night, sweet friend:
Thy love ne'er alter, till thy sweet life end!

Lysander   Amen, amen, to that fair prayer say I;
65   And then, end life, when I end loyalty!
Here is my bed; sleep give thee all his rest.

Lysander   Dearest, you are weary with wandering through the wood. Frankly, I'm lost. We'll rest, Hermia, if you agree, and wait till daylight when travelling is easier.

Hermia   That's best, Lysander. Find yourself a bed. I'll sleep here on this bank. [*She settles down on the grass*]

Lysander   One turf will serve as a pillow for us both. Our hearts are one: Our bed is one. One vow of love unites our two hearts – [*He chooses a spot close to her*]

Hermia   No, good Lysander. For my sake, my dear, lie further away. Don't lie so near.

Lysander   Oh, I speak in all innocence, dearest, so don't get me wrong. Love knows what's really meant when lovers talk. My meaning was that my heart and yours are so closely knit that we share one heart. Since we have sworn our love for each other, our hearts are, as it were bound together; that's the single truth that unites the two of us. So don't deny me bed-room at your side. By lying that way, Hermia, I can't lie in the other sense of the word!

Hermia   Lysander plays with words very charmingly. Shame on my manners and my self-esteem if I seemed to suggest that you lied! But, gentle friend, in the name of love and good manners, lie further off, out of common decency. About as far a distance as would be thought proper between a virtuous bachelor and a single girl. [*She indicates a suitable place*] This far apart. Good night, sweet friend. May your love never change as long as you live!

Lysander   Amen, amen to that prayer, say I! If I broke faith, I'd deserve to die. Here's my bed. Sleep tight.

Hermia   With half that wish, the wisher's eyes be pressed.

[*They sleep*]

[*Enter* **Puck**]

Puck   Through the forest have I gone,
But Athenian found I none
70 On whose eyes I might approve
This flower's force in stirring love.
Night and silence: who is here?
Weeds of Athens he doth wear:
This is he my master said
75 Despised the Athenian maid:
And here the maiden, sleeping sound,
On the dank and dirty ground.
Pretty soul, she durst not lie
Near this lack-love, this kill-courtesy.
80 Churl, upon thy eyes I throw
All the power this charm doth owe.
When thou wak'st let love forbid
Sleep his seat on thy eyelid.
So wake when I am gone;
85 For I must now to Oberon.

[*Exit*]

[*Enter* **Demetrius** *and* **Helena**, *running*]

Helena   Stay, though thou kill me, sweet Demetrius.

Demetrius   I charge thee hence, and do not haunt me thus.

Helena   O wilt thou darkling leave me? Do not so.

Hermia   I'll share that wish with you.

[*They sleep*]

[**Puck** *enters*]

Puck   Through the forest I have been:
   But no Athenian have I seen
   On whose eyes to try the power
   Of this love-begetting flower.
   Night and silence. Who is there?
   Athen's clothing is his wear.
   My master guides me. Surely this
   Is he who hates the Athens miss?
   And here's the maiden, sleeping sound
   On the damp and dirty ground.
   Pretty soul, she dare not stretch
   Near this kill-joy; loveless wretch!
   Peasant! On your eyes I place
   All the power these charms embrace.

[*He places drops on* **Lysander's** *eyelids*]

   When you wake up, love forbids
   That you should ever close your lids.
   So waken after I have gone
   For I must go to Oberon.

[*He leaves*]

[**Demetrius** *and* **Helena** *enter, running*]

Helena   Stop, even if it's to kill me, Demetrius!

Demetrius   Don't haunt me like this!

Helena   Oh, will you leave me alone in the dark! Please
   don't!

90 **Demetrius**   Stay on thy peril; I alone will go.

[*Exit* **Demetrius**]

Helena   O, I am out of breath, in this fond chase!
The more my prayer, the lesser is my grace.
Happy is Hermia, wheresoe'er she lies,
For she hath blessed and attractive eyes.
95 How came her eyes so bright? Not with salt tears:
If so, my eyes are oftener washed than hers.
No, no, I am as ugly as a bear;
For beasts that meet me run away for fear.
Therefore no marvel though Demetrius
100 Do, as a monster, fly my presence thus.
What wicked and dissembling glass of mine
Made me compare with Hermia's sphery eyne?
But who is here? Lysander on the ground!
Dead or asleep? I see no blood, no wound.
105 Lysander, if you live, good sir, awake!

Lysander   [*waking*] And run through fire I will for thy
sweet sake!
Transparent Helena! Nature shows art,
That through thy bosom makes me see thy heart.
110 Where is Demetrius? O how fit a word
Is that vile name, to perish on my sword!

Helena   Do not say so, Lysander; say not so:
What though he love your Hermia? Lord, what though?
Yet Hermia still loves you; then be content.

115 **Lysander**   Content with Hermia? No, I do repent
The tedious minutes I with her have spent.
Not Hermia, but Helena I love:
Who will not change a raven for a dove?
The will of man is by his reason swayed;
120 And reason says you are the worthier maid.

Demetrius   Stay, and take your chance! I'll go alone.

[*He rushes off*]

Helena   Oh, I'm out of breath after all this silly chasing.
The more I pray, the less I'm granted. How happy is
Hermia, wherever she is, because she is blessed with
attractive eyes. How did her eyes come to be so bright?
Not with salt tears: my eyes are more often bathed in
them than hers. No, no: I'm as repulsive as a bear,
because beasts who meet me run away in fright.
Therefore no wonder Demetrius runs away from me as if
I'm some monster. What distorting mirror of mine
compared my eyes with Hermia's starry ones? [*She
notices the sleeping* **Lysander**] Who's this? Lysander, on
the ground? Is he dead, or sleeping? I can't see blood, or
a wound. [*She shakes him*] Lysander – if you're alive,
good sir, wake up!

Lysander   [*waking up, face to face with* **Helena**] And I'd
run through fire for your sweet sake! Helena the crystal-
clear! Nature is clever: I can see the loving heart that lies
within your bosom! Where is Demetrius? That vile name
could not be bettered as a victim of my sword!

Helena   Don't say that, Lysander! Don't say that!
[*mistaking his reasons*] What if he does love your
Hermia? What does it matter, in heaven's name? Hermia
still loves you. Be content with that.

Lysander   Content with Hermia? No! I regret the tedious
moments I've spent with her. I love Helena – not
Hermia. Who wouldn't exchange a raven for a dove? The
mind of man is influenced by reason. Reason says you
are the more attractive girl. Growing things don't ripen

Things growing are not ripe until their season;
So I, being young, till now ripe not to reason;
And touching now the point of human skill,
Reason becomes the marshal to my will,
125   And leads me to your eyes, where I o'erlook
Love's stories, written in love's richest book.

Helena   Wherefore was I to this keen mockery born?
When at your hands did I deserve this scorn?
Is't not enough, is't not enough, young man,
130   That I did never, no, nor never can
Deserve a sweet look from Demetrius' eye,
But you must flout my insufficiency?
Good troth, you do me wrong, good sooth, you do,
In such disdainful manner me to woo.
135   But fare you well; perforce I must confess
I thought you lord of more true gentleness.
O, that a lady of one man refused
Should of another therefore be abused!

[*Exit*]

Lysander   She sees not Hermia. Hermia, sleep thou there;
140   And never mayst thou come Lysander near!
For, as a surfeit of the sweetest things
The deepest loathing to the stomach brings,
Or as the heresies that men do leave,
Are hated most of those they did deceive;
145   So thou, my surfeit, and my heresy,
Of all be hated, but the most of me.
And, all my powers, address your love and might
To honour Helen, and to be her knight!

[*Exit*]

till the proper time. Till now, being young, I haven't been ready to be guided by reason. Now I've matured, reason guides my behaviour, and leads me to your eyes, where I see volumes of love richly inscribed.

Helena Why was I born to be mocked so unmercifully like this? What have I done to deserve your scorn? Isn't it enough, isn't it enough, young man, that I've never had, nor ever will have, a kind look from Demetrius, without you mocking me for my deficiencies? Honestly, you do me an injustice, you really do, to woo me in such a disrespectful manner. Goodbye. I really must say that I thought you were more of a gentleman. Oh, that a lady rejected by one man should be abused by another!

[*She runs off, distressed*]

Lysander She didn't notice Hermia. Hermia, sleep on where you are, and may you never come near Lysander! Because, just as too much sweetness leads to loathing – or just as converts most hate what they formerly believed – so you, my surfeit, my wrongheadedness! – may you be universally hated, but especially by me. My entire being I now dedicate to honouring Helena and serving her faithfully.

[*He follows her*]

Hermia   [*waking*] Help me, Lysander, help me! Do thy
    best
150   To pluck this crawling serpent from my breast!
    Ay me, for pity! what a dream was here!
    Lysander, look, how I do quake with fear.
    Methought a serpent eat my heart away,
    And you sat smiling at his cruel prey.
155   Lysander! what, removed? Lysander! lord!
    What, out of hearing? Gone? no sound, no word?
    Alack, where are you? Speak, and if you hear:
    Speak, of all loves; I swoon almost with fear.
    No? Then I will perceive you are not nigh.
160   Either death or you I'll find immediately.

[*Exit*]

Hermia   [*waking from a nightmare*] Help me, Lysander!
Help me! Try to remove this snake that's crawling on my
breast! Oh dear! Have pity on me! What a dream I've
had! Lysander, see how I'm trembling with fright. I
thought a serpent ate my heart away, and you sat smiling
as he preyed on me. Lysander! [*She realises he is not
there*] What, gone away? Lysander! My Lord! What, can't
you hear me! Gone? No sound? No word? Alas, where
are you? If you can hear me, speak! Speak, in the name
of love! I almost faint from fear. [*There is silence*] No?
Then you can't be nearby. I'll meet my death, or you,
without delay.

[*She goes, leaving* **Titania** *alone, and asleep*]

Act three

Scene 1

Titania *sleeps. Enter* **Quince, Snug, Bottom, Flute, Snout** *and* **Starveling**.

Bottom   Are we all met?

Quince   Pat, pat; and here's a marvellous convenient place for our rehearsal. This green plot shall be our stage, this hawthorn-brake our tiring-house, and we will do it in
5   action, as we will do it before the Duke.

Bottom   Peter Quince!

Quince   What sayest thou, bully Bottom?

Bottom   There are things in this comedy of Pyramus and Thisbe that will never please. First, Pyramus must draw a
10   sword to kill himself; which the ladies cannot abide. How answer you that?

Snout   By'r lakin, a parlous fear.

Starveling   I believe we must leave the killing out, when all is done.

15 **Bottom**   Not a whit; I have a device to make all well. Write me a prologue, and let the prologue seem to say, we will do no harm with our swords, and that Pyramus is not killed indeed; and for the more better assurance, tell them that I Pyramus am not Pyramus, but Bottom the weaver;
20   this will put them out of fear.

Quince   Well, we will have such a prologue; and it shall be written in eight and six.

Act three

Scene 1

Quince, Bottom, Snug, Flute, Snout *and* **Starveling** *enter the glade.*

Bottom   Are we all here?

Quince   Right on time. And here's a marvellously suitable place for our rehearsal. This grassy patch will be our stage, this hawthorn thicket our dressing-room, and we'll go through the moves just as we'll do it before the Duke.

Bottom   Peter Quince?

Quince   Yes, brother Bottom?

Bottom   There are things in this comedy of Pyramus and Thisbe that won't be liked. First, Pyramus has to draw a sword to kill himself, which will upset the ladies. What do you say to that?

Snout   By heck: that's really worrying.

Starveling   I think we'll have to leave the killing out, when all's said and done.

Bottom   Not at all. I've got a way round it. Write a prologue, and in the prologue hint that we won't do any harm with our swords, and that Pyramus isn't really killed. To make doubly sure, tell them that I'm not Pyramus, but Bottom the weaver. This will put their minds at rest.

Quince   Well, we'll have such a prologue. It'll be in verse: eight beats in the first line, six in the next.

Bottom   No, make it two more; let it be written in eight
and eight.

25 **Snout**   Will not the ladies be afeard of the lion?

Starveling   I fear it, I promise you.

Bottom   Masters, you ought to consider with yourself; to
bring in, God shield us, a lion among ladies is a most
dreadful thing: for there is not a more fearful wild fowl
30   than your lion living; and we ought to look to't.

Snout   Therefore another prologue must tell he is not a
lion.

Bottom   Nay, you must name his name, and half his face
must be seen through the lion's neck; and he himself must
35   speak through, saying thus, or to the same defect: 'Ladies',
or 'Fair ladies', 'I would wish you' or 'I would request
you', or 'I would entreat you, not to fear, not to tremble:
my life for yours. If you think I come hither as a lion, it
were pity of my life. No, I am no such thing; I am a man
40   as other men are'; and there indeed let him name his name,
and tell them plainly he is Snug the joiner.

Quince   Well, it shall be so: but there is two hard things,
that is, to bring the moonlight into a chamber; for, you
know, Pyramus and Thisbe meet by moonlight.

45 **Snout**   Doth the moon shine that night we play our play?

Bottom   A calendar, a calendar; look in the almanac; find
out moonshine, find out moonshine.

Quince   Yes, it doth shine that night.

Bottom   Why, then may you leave a casement of the great
50   chamber window, where we play, open, and the moon
may shine in at the casement.

Bottom   No. Make it two more. Write it eight and eight.

Snout   Won't the ladies be scared of the lion?

Starveling   It will scare me, I can tell you.

Bottom   Gentlemen, you'd better think about this. To bring in a lion – god help us! – amongst ladies is an awful thing to do. There's no more terrifying wild bird than your lion in all creation. We'd better look into this.

Snout   So we'll have to have another prologue, saying he's not really a lion.

Bottom   Not only that, you must name him by name, and half his face must be seen through his lion's mask, and he must speak in person through it. He can say, or something to the same defect, 'Ladies', or 'Beautiful ladies' – 'I would wish you', or 'I would request you', or 'I would entreat you not to be afraid, not to tremble upon my life! If you thought I came here as a lion, I'd be mortified. No – I'm no such thing. I'm just an ordinary man.' And then he can name his name, and tell them straight that he's Snug the joiner.

Quince   Well, all right then. But there's two problems: how to bring the moonlight into the room – because, you know, Pyramus and Thisbe meet by moonlight –

Snout   Will the moon be shining on the night we perform the play?

Bottom   Get a calendar, a calendar. Look up the almanac. Find out when there's a moon, when there's a moon . . .

Quince   [*looking it up*] Yes – there's a moon that night.

Bottom   Well, then you can leave a window open in the main hall, where we perform, and the moon can shine in at it.

Quince   Ay, or else one must come in with a bush of thorns
and a lantern, and say he comes to disfigure or to present
the person of moonshine. Then there is another thing; we
55   must have a wall in the great chamber; for Pyramus and
Thisbe, says the story, did talk through the chink of a
wall.

Snout   You can never bring in a wall. What say you,
Bottom?

60   **Bottom**   Some man or other must present Wall; and let him
have some plaster, or some loam, or some rough-cast about
him, to signify wall; or let him hold his fingers thus; and
through that cranny shall Pyramus and Thisbe whisper.

Quince   If that may be, then all is well. Come, sit down,
65   every mother's son, and rehearse your parts. Pyramus, you
begin; when you have spoken your speech, enter into that
brake; and so every one according to his cue.

[*Enter* **Puck** *behind*]

Puck   What hempen home-spuns have we swaggering here,
So near the cradle of the fairy queen?
70   What, a play toward? I'll be an auditor;
An actor too, perhaps, if I see cause.

Quince   Speak, Pyramus. Thisbe, stand forth.

Bottom   Thisbe, the flowers of odious savours sweet.

Quince   Odours, odours.

75   **Bottom**   Odours savours sweet;
So hath thy breath, my dearest Thisbe dear.

Quince   Yes, or else someone will have to come in with a
thornbush and a lantern, and say he comes to
importunate, or represent, the character of moonshine.
Then there's another thing. We must have a wall in the
main hall, because Pyramus and Thisbe, according to the
story, talked through a chink in the wall.

Snout   You'll never be able to bring in a wall. What do you
think, Bottom?

Bottom   Some man or other must represent the wall. He'll
have to have some plaster, or some loam, or some
roughcast over him, to suggest 'wall'. Or he can hold his
fingers like this [*he makes a V to demonstrate*] and
through that gap Pyramus and Thisbe can whisper.

Quince   If we can do that, we've nothing to worry about.
Right. Sit down, every mother's son, and rehearse your
parts. Pyramus, you begin. When you've said your lines,
go into the thicket. Likewise everyone else, according
to his cue.

[**Puck** *enters unseen*]

Puck   What rough-clothed rustics have we swaggering
here, so near to where the fairy queen's asleep?
What – a play imminent? I'll be a member of the
audience, and an actor too, perhaps, if I get a chance.

Quince   Speak, Pyramus. Thisbe, stand forward.

Bottom   [*playing* **Pyramus**] Thisbe, the flowers have odious
sweet smells –

Quince   [*prompting*] Odorous, odorous . . .

Bottom   Odorous sweet smells;
So has your breath, my dearest Thisbe dear.

But hark, a voice! stay thou but here a while,
And by and by I will to thee appear.

[*Exit behind*]

Puck   A stranger Pyramus than e'er played here!

80 **Flute**   Must I speak now?

Quince   Ay, marry, must you; for you must understand, he
goes but to see a noise that he heard, and is to come again.

Flute   Most radiant Pyramus, most lily-white of hue,
Of colour like the red rose on triumphant briar,
85   Most brisky juvenal, and eke most lovely Jew,
As truest horse, that yet would never tire.
I'll meet thee, Pyramus, at Ninny's tomb.

Quince   'Ninus' tomb', man! Why, you must not speak that
yet; that you answer to Pyramus. You speak all your part
90   at once, cues and all. Pyramus, enter: your cue is past; it is
'never tire'.

Flute   O, – As true as truest horse, that yet would never
tire.

[*Re-enter* **Bottom** *wearing an ass's head*]

Bottom   If I were fair, Thisbe, I were only thine.

95 **Quince**   O montrous! O strange! We are haunted; pray,
masters, fly! masters, help!

But listen! A voice! Stay here a little while,
And by and by, to you I'll reappear.

[*He goes, dramatically*]

Puck   The weirdest Pyramus ever!

Flute   Should I speak now?

Quince   Yes, you must. You see, he's only gone to see a
noise he's heard, and he'll be back.

Flute   [*as* **Thisbe**]
Most radiant Pyramus, most lily-white of hue;
Of colour like the red rose on triumphant briar,
Most lively lad, and also most lovely Jew;
You faithful horse, that never seems to tire.
I'll meet you, Pyramus, at Ninny's tomb.

Quince   [*exploding*] Ninus's tomb, man! But you mustn't
say that yet! That's your answer to Pyramus! You're
speaking all your part at once, cues and all. Pyramus,
enter! You've missed your cue. It's 'never seems to tire'.

Flute   [*as* **Thisbe**]
Oh, you faithful horse, that never seems to tire.

[**Bottom** *returns. He is wearing an ass's head, and does
not know it*]

Bottom   [*as* **Pyramus**]
If I were beautiful, Thisbe . . . [*He pauses and starts again*]
If I were, beautiful Thisbe, I'd be yours alone . . .

Quince   [*reacting to* **Bottom's** *unexpected appearance*]
How monstrous! How strange! We're haunted! Please,
gentlemen, run! [*For a moment they can't, they are so
afraid*] Gentlemen! Help!

85

[*Exeunt all but* **Bottom** *and* **Puck**]

Puck   I'll follow you, I'll lead you about a round,
Through bog, through bush, through brake, through briar;
Sometime a horse I'll be, sometime a hound,
100   A hog, a headless bear, sometime a fire;
And neigh, and bark, and grunt, and roar, and burn,
Like horse, hound, hog, bear, fire, at every turn.

[*Exit*]

Bottom   Why do they run away? This is a knavery of them
to make me afeard.

[*Enter* **Snout**]

105   **Snout**   O Bottom, thou art changed! What do I see on thee?

Bottom   What do you see? You see an ass-head of your
own, do you?

[*Exit* **Snout**]

[*Enter* **Quince**]

Quince   Bless thee Bottom, bless thee! Thou art translated!

[*Exit*]

Bottom   I see their knavery: this is to make an ass of me, to
110   fright me, if they could; but I will not stir from this place,
do what they can. I will walk up and down here, and I
will sing, that they shall hear I am not afraid.

[*Everyone but* **Bottom** *and* **Puck** *runs off*]

Puck   I'll follow you! I'll lead you round and round –
Through bog, through bush, through brake, through briar!
Sometimes I'll be a horse, sometimes a hound
A hog, a headless bear, or else a fire!
I'll neigh, and bark, and grunt, and roar, and burn
Like horse, hound, hog, bear, fire, at every turn!

[**Puck** *chases after them*]

Bottom   Why are they running away? This is a joke, to
frighten me.

[**Snout** *returns*]

Snout   Oh Bottom! You've changed! What's that I see
on you! [*He points to the ass's head*]

Bottom   What do you see? You see an ass's head like
yours, do you?

[**Snout** *runs off*]

[**Quince** *comes back*]

Quince   Bless you, Bottom, bless you! You've been
transformed!

[*He runs off too*]

Bottom   I see their game. This is to make an ass of me, to
frighten me, if they can! But I won't move from this
place, however hard they try. I'll walk up and down here.
I'll sing, so they'll know I'm not afraid:

[*Sings*]   *The ousel cock, so black of hue,*
             With orange-tawny bill,
115   *The throstle with his note so true,*
             The wren with little quill –

Titania   [*waking*] What angel wakes me from my flowery
bed?

Bottom   [*Sings*]   *The finch, the sparrow, and the lark,*
120   *The plain-song cuckoo grey;*
             Whose note full many a man doth mark,
             And dares not answer nay.

For indeed, who would set his wit to so foolish a bird?
Who would give a bird the lie, though he cry 'cuckoo'
125 never so?

Titania   I pray thee, gentle mortal, sing again;
Mine ear is much enamoured of thy note;
So is mine eye enthralled to thy shape;
And thy fair virtue's force perforce doth move me
130 On the first view, to say, to swear, I love thee.

Bottom   Methinks, mistress, you should have little reason
for that: and to say the truth, reason and love keep little
company together nowadays. The more the pity that some
honest neighbours will not make them friends. Nay, I can
135 gleek upon occasion.

Titania   Thou art as wise as thou art beautiful.

Bottom   Not so, neither; but if I had wit enough to get out
of this wood, I have enough to serve mine own turn.

Titania   Out of this wood do not desire to go;
140 Thou shalt remain here, whether thou wilt or no.
I am a spirit of no common rate;
The summer still doth tend upon my state,
And I do love thee; therefore, go with me.

The blackbird that's so black of hue
With orange-tawny bill,
The thrush that has a song so true,
The wren with tiny trill –

Titania   [*waking up*] What angel wakes me from my bed of flowers?

Bottom   [*singing on*] *The finch, the sparrow and the lark*
The two-note cuckoo grey
Whose song's a message all men mark
Because they daren't say 'nay'.

Indeed, who'd match his wits against such a stupid bird? Who'd bother to contradict what it said, however often it cried 'cuckoo'?

Titania   Gentle mortal – please sing again! I loved listening to your song. Your looks fascinate me. Your forceful personality compels me to declare that I'm in love with you, at first sight.

Bottom   You've little reason to say that, I think, madam; but then, let's face it, reason and love don't go together much nowadays. Some good people won't link the two, more's the pity. I can say the right thing when I have to!

Titania   You are as wise as you are beautiful!

Bottom   I don't really think so. If I had enough brains to get out of this wood, that would do me nicely.

Titania   Out of the wood do not desire to go –
You shall remain, whether you will or no.
I am a spirit of some royalty
The summer season owes me loyalty.
I love you truly. Therefore, let's proceed.

145 I'll give thee fairies to attend on thee;
And they shall fetch thee jewels from the deep,
And sing, while thou on pressed flowers dost sleep:
And I will purge thy mortal grossness so
That thou shalt like an airy spirit go.
Peaseblossom, Cobweb, Moth, and Mustardseed!

[*Enter four* **Fairies: Peaseblossom, Cobweb, Moth** *and* **Mustardseed**]

Peaseblossom Ready.

Cobweb And I.

Moth And I.

150 **Mustardseed** And I.

All Where
shall we go?

Titania Be kind and courteous to this gentleman:
Hop in his walks, and gambol in his eyes;
Feed him with apricocks and dewberries,
155 With purple grapes, green figs, and mulberries;
The honey-bags steal from the humble-bees,
And for night-tapers crop their waxen thighs,
And light them at the fiery glow-worm's eyes,
To have my love to bed, and to arise;
160 And pluck the wings from painted butterflies
To fan the moonbeams from his sleeping eyes;
Nod to him, elves, and do him courtesies.

Peaseblossom Hail, mortal!

Cobweb Hail!

Moth Hail!

Mustardseed Hail!

My fairies will provide your every need.
They'll fetch you jewels from the ocean deep
And sing while beds of flowers soothe your sleep.
I'll take away your mortal features:
You'll be light – just like us fairy creatures.
Peaseblossom! Cobweb! Moth and Mustardseed!

[*Four tiny* **Fairies** *enter*]

Peaseblossom   Ready!

Cobweb   And me!

Moth   And me!

Mustardseed   And me!

All   Where shall we go?

Titania   Be kind and courteous to this gentleman:
Dance at his side, in full view of his eyes;
Feed him with apricots and blackberries;
With purple grapes, green figs and mulberries.
Steal honey-bags from all the bumble-bees;
And candles make from wax that's on their knees;
And light them from the glow-worm's fiery eyes,
To guide my love in safety where he lies.
And pluck the wings from coloured butterflies
To fan the moonbeams from his sleeping eyes.
Bow to him elves, and do him courtesies.

Peaseblossom   Hail, mortal!

Cobweb   Hail!

Moth   Hail!

Mustardseed   Hail!

Bottom   I cry your worship's mercy heartily; I beseech your
165   worship's name?

Cobweb   Cobweb.

Bottom   I shall desire you of more acquaintance, good
Master Cobweb: if I cut my finger, I shall make bold with
you. Your name, honest gentleman?

170 **Peaseblossom**   Peaseblossom.

Bottom   I pray you, commend me to Mistress Squash, your
mother, and to Master Peascod, your father. Good Master
Peaseblossom, I shall desire you of more acquaintance too.
Your name, I beseech you, sir?

175 **Mustardseed**   Mustardseed.

Bottom   Good Master Mustardseed, I know your patience
well. That same cowardly, giant-like ox-beef hath
devoured many a gentleman of your house. I promise you,
your kindred hath made my eyes water ere now. I desire
180   you of more acquaintance, good Master Mustardseed.

Titania   Come, wait upon him, lead him to my bower.
The moon, methinks, looks with a watery eye,
And when she weeps, weeps every little flower,
Lamenting some enforced chastity.
185   Tie up my love's tongue, bring him silently.

[Exeunt]

Bottom   Greetings to your worship. [*To* **Cobweb**] May I know your worship's name?

Cobweb   Cobweb.

Bottom   I'd like to get to know you better, good Master Cobweb. If I cut my finger, I'll use you to stop the bleeding. [*To* **Peaseblossom**] Your name, my good sir?

Peaseblossom   Peaseblossom.

Bottom   My regards to Mrs Squash, your mother, and Mr Peascod, your father. Master Peascod, sir: I'd like to be better acquainted with you, too. [*To* **Mustardseed**] Your name, please sir?

Mustardseed   Mustardseed.

Bottom   Mr Mustardseed, I know very well how long-suffering you are. Those cowardly, giant-sized sides of beef have eaten up many of your relations. They've made my eyes water many a time, I can tell you. We must see more of each other, Mr Mustardseed.

Titania   [*to the* **Fairies**] Come – wait upon him, and escort him to my arbour. The moon is misty-eyed, and when she weeps, so does every little flower in grief for violated chastity. [**Bottom** *gives vent to a noisy bray*] Tie up my love's tongue. Lead him in silently.

Scene 2

Another part of the wood. Enter **Oberon**.

Oberon   I wonder if Titania be awaked;
Then, what it was that next came in her eye,
Which she must dote on in extremity.

[*Enter* **Puck**]

Here comes my messenger. How now, mad spirit!
5   What night-rule now about this haunted grove?

Puck   My mistress with a monster is in love.
Near to her close and consecrated bower,
While she was in her dull and sleeping hour,
A crew of patches, rude mechanicals,
10   That work for bread upon Athenian stalls,
Were met together to rehearse a play
Intended for great Theseus' nuptial-day.
The shallowest thick-skin of that barren sort,
Who Pyramus presented, in their sport
15   Forsook his scene and entered in a brake;
When I did him at this advantage take,
An ass's nole I fixed on his head.
Anon his Thisbe must be answered,
And forth my mimic comes. When they him spy,
20   As wild geese that the creeping fowler eye,
Or russet-pated choughs, many in sort,
Rising and cawing at the gun's report,
Sever themselves and madly sweep the sky,
So at his sight, away his fellows fly;
25   And at our stamp, here o'er and o'er one falls;
He 'murder' cries, and help from Athens calls.
Their sense thus weak, lost with their fears thus strong,

Scene 2

Another part of the wood. **Oberon** *enters*

Oberon   I wonder if Titania is awake? And what it was that
she saw first, which she must love devotedly.

[**Puck** *enters*]

Here comes my messenger. Well now, zany spirit. What
night-larking is there in this haunted grove?

Puck   My mistress is in love with a monster! A gang of
yokels – common working men, who earn their livings in
Athenian workshops – met together near her secret
hallowed arbour while she was sleeping, in order to
rehearse a play intended for great Theseus's wedding-
day. The most stupid thick-head of that ignorant lot, who
played the part of Pyramus in their entertainment, left the
scene and went into a thicket. Taking advantage of this,
I fixed an ass's head on him. Soon after which his Thisbe
spoke his cue, so on my so-called actor comes. When
they set eyes on him, they flew off like wild geese
who've spotted a bird-catcher, or brown headed
jackdaws, scattering and sweeping dementedly across
the sky, rising and cawing at the firing of a gun. And
hearing the stamp of my feet, one of them tumbles head
over heels. 'Murder!' he shouts, and calls for help from
Athens. Their wits so scattered, distracted by their fears,

Made senseless things begin to do them wrong;
For briars and thorns at their apparel snatch;
30 Some sleeves, some hats; from yielders all things catch.
I led them on in this distracted fear,
And left sweet Pyramus translated there;
When in that moment, so it came to pass,
Titania waked, and straightway loved an ass.

35 **Oberon** This falls out better than I could devise.
But hast thou yet latched the Athenian's eyes
With the love-juice, as I did bid thee do?

Puck I took him sleeping – that is finished too –
And the Athenian woman by his side;
40 That, when he waked, of force she must be eyed.

[*Enter* **Demetrius** *and* **Hermia**]

Oberon Stand close: this is the same Athenian.

Puck This is the woman, but not this the man.

Demetrius O, why rebuke you him that loves you so?
Lay breath so bitter on your bitter foe.

45 **Hermia** Now I but chide, but I should use thee worse,
For thou, I fear, hast given me cause to curse.
If thou hast slain Lysander in his sleep,
Being o'er shoes in blood, plunge in the deep,
And kill me too.
50 The sun was not so true unto the day
As he to me. Would he have stolen away
From sleeping Hermia? I'll believe as soon
This whole earth may be bored, and that the moon
May through the centre creep, and so displease
55 Her brother's noontide with the Antipodes.
It cannot be but thou hast murdered him;
So should a murderer look; so dead, so grim.

inanimate objects begin to do them harm. Briars
and thorns tear their clothes, their sleeves, their
hats – everything catches when people lose control. I led
them on in their panic, and left 'sweet Pyramus' there
with his new appearance. Just at that moment, it so
happened Titania woke – and immediately she fell in love
with an ass!

Oberon I couldn't have planned it better! But have you
moistened the Athenian's eyes with the love-juice, as I
told you to?

Puck That's done too. I found him asleep with the
Athenian woman by his side. He couldn't miss seeing her
when he woke up.

[**Demetrius** *and* **Hermia** *enter*]

Oberon Hide yourself. This is the Athenian I meant.

Puck This is the woman – but this isn't the man!

[*They take cover*]

Demetrius Oh, why do you scold a man who loves you so?
Keep such bitter words for your bitterest enemy!

Hermia I'm only ticking you off now, but I should be
more severe: you may, I fear, have given me reason to
curse you. If you have killed Lysander in his sleep, since
you're already steeped in blood, go the whole hog and kill
me too! The sun was not as faithful to the day as he was
to me. Would he have crept away from his sleeping
Hermia? I'd just as soon believe the earth could have a
hole drilled through the middle for the moon to creep
through, and muddle up mid-day on the other side of the
world. You must have murdered him. You look like a
murderer, so deathly, so grim.

Demetrius   So should the murdered look; and so should I,
Pierced through the heart with your stern cruelty:
60   Yet you, the murderer, look as bright, as clear
As yonder Venus in her glimmering sphere.

Hermia   What's this to my Lysander? Where is he?
Ah, good Demetrius, wilt thou give him me?

Demetrius   I had rather give his carcass to my hounds.

65 **Hermia**   Out, dog! out, cur! thou drivest me past the
bounds
Of maiden's patience. Hast thou slain him, then?
Henceforth be never numbered among men!
O, once tell true; tell true, even for my sake!
70   Durst thou have looked upon him, being awake?
And hast thou killed him sleeping? O brave touch!
Could not a worm, an adder do so much?
An adder did it: for with doubler tongue
Than thine, thou serpent, never adder stung!

75 **Demetrius**   You spend your passion on a misprised mood:
I am not guilty of Lysander's blood;
Nor is he dead, for aught that I can tell.

Hermia   I pray thee tell me then that he is well.

Demetrius   An if I could, what should I get therefore?

80 **Hermia**   A privilege, never to see me more.
And from thy hated presence part I so:
See me no more, whether he be dead or no.

[*Exit*]

Demetrius   There is no following her in this fierce vein;
Here therefore for a while I will remain.
85   So sorrow's heaviness doth heavier grow

Demetrius That's how the murdered look, and how I
should: stabbed through the heart by your stern cruelty.
But you, the murderer, look as bright and clear as the
star Venus, up there in the shining sky.

Hermia What's this got to do with my Lysander? Where is
he? Oh, good Demetrius – will you give him back to me?

Demetrius I'd rather give his carcase to my hounds!

Hermia You dog! You cur! You push me beyond a maiden's
natural patience. Have you killed him, then? From now
on, don't count yourself as human! Once and for all – tell
the truth! For my sake, tell the truth! Would you have
dared to face him, if he'd been awake? Did you kill him
sleeping? Oh, very brave! Couldn't a worm, couldn't a
snake, have done as much? A snake did do it! No snake
ever stung with such a forked tongue as yours, you
serpent!

Demetrius Your anger's misplaced. I'm not guilty of killing
Lysander. Not that he's dead, for all I know.

Hermia Tell me he's all right then, will you?

Demetrius Even if I could, what would I get in return?

Hermia The privilege of never seeing me again. And on
that I'll quit your hated presence. Don't see me again,
whether he's dead or not.

[She goes]

Demetrius There's no following her in this angry mood. I'll
stay here, therefore, for a while. The weight of sorrow

For debt that bankrupt sleep doth sorrow owe,
Which now in some slight measure it will pay,
If for his tender here I make some stay.

[*He lies down and sleeps*]

Oberon What hast thou done? Thou hast mistaken quite,
90 And laid the love-juice on some true-love's sight.
Of thy misprision must perforce ensue
Some true love turned, and not a false turned true.

Puck Then fate o'er-rules, that, one man holding troth,
A million fail, confounding oath on oath.

95 **Oberon** About the wood go swifter than the wind,
And Helena of Athens look thou find.
All fancy-sick she is and pale of cheer
With signs of love that cost the fresh blood dear.
By some illusion see thou bring her here;
100 I'll charm his eyes against she do appear.

Puck I go, I go, look how I go!
Swifter than arrow from the Tartar's bow.

[*Exit*]

Oberon Flower of this purple dye,
Hit with Cupid's archery,
105 Sink in apple of his eye.
When his love he doth espy,
Let her shine as gloriously
As the Venus of the sky.
When thou wak'st, if she be by,
110 Beg of her for remedy.

[*Enter* **Puck**]

increases, made worse by loss of sleep. I'll put that partly right by taking a nap here.

[*He lies down and sleeps*]

Oberon   [*coming forward*] What have you done? You got it all wrong! You've put the love-juice on the eyes of some genuine lover. Your bungling must result in upsetting true love, not putting false love right.

Puck   Fate has decided that, for every man who keeps his word, a million break their promises, one pledge cancelling out another.

Oberon   Go round the wood swifter than the wind, and see you find Helena of Athens. She's very love-sick, and pale-faced, sighing at the expense of her good colour. Trick her into coming here. I'll love-juice his eyes ready for her coming.

Puck   I go, I go: look how I go! Swifter than an arrow shot from a Tartar's bow.

[*He goes*]

Oberon   [*squeezing the juice on* **Demetrius's** *eyes*]

> Flower with this purple dye,
> Strike with Cupid's accuracy!
> Pierce the pupil of his eye.
> When his love he first does see,
> Let her shine as gloriously
> As the Venus in the sky.
> When you wake, if she is near,
> Beg that she will be your dear.

[**Puck** *returns*]

Puck   Captain of our fairy band,
　　　Helena is here at hand,
　　　And the youth, mistook by me,
　　　Pleading for a lover's fee.
115　Shall we their fond pageant see?
　　　Lord, what fools these mortals be!

Oberon   Stand aside: the noise they make
　　　Will cause Demetrius to wake.

Puck   Then will two at once woo one;
120　That must needs be sport alone;
　　　And those things do best please me
　　　That befall preposterously.

　　　　　　　　　　　　　　　　　[*They stand aside*]

[*Enter* **Lysander** *and* **Helena**]

Lysander   Why should you think that I should woo in
　　　scorn?
125　Scorn and derision never come in tears:
　　　Look when I vow I weep; and vows so born
　　　In their nativity all truth appears.
　　　How can these things in me seem scorn to you,
　　　Bearing the badge of faith to prove them true?

130 **Helena**   You do advance your cunning more and more.
　　　When truth kills troth, O devilish-holy fray!
　　　These vows are Hermia's: will you give her o'er?
　　　Weigh oath with oath, and you will nothing weigh.
　　　Your vows to her and me, put in two scales,
135　Will even weigh; and both as light as tales.

Lysander   I had no judgement when to her I swore.

Puck   Captain of our fairy band
Helena is here at hand,
And the youth mistook by me,
Pleading that he loved may be.
Shall we their performance see?
Lord – what fools these mortals be!

Oberon   Stand aside. The noise they make
Will cause Demetrius to wake.

Puck   Then will two men love one girl –
That will put things in a whirl!
The sort of things that best please me
Happen quite ridiculously!

[*They watch from a distance*]

[**Lysander** *and* **Helena** *enter*]

Lysander   Why do you think I love you mockingly? Tears
don't go with scorn and derision. Whenever I vow my
love, I weep: vows born in tears are always honest. How
can these feelings of mine seem scornful to you, when
they carry the tearful stamp of authenticity?

Helena   Your cunning increases all the time! When a
truthful vow to one of us means that a vow to the other
is a lie, that's devilishly honest! You owe these vows to
Hermia. Have you thrown her over? If one of your vows
cancels out another, it means you have no integrity. Put
your vows to her on one scale, and your vows to me on
the other, and they'd balance. They'd be featherweight!

Lysander   I didn't know what I was doing when I swore my
love to her.

Helena   Nor none, in my mind, now you give her o'er.

Lysander   Demetrius loves her, and he loves not you.

Demetrius [*waking*] O Helen, goddess, nymph, perfect,
140   divine,
To what, my love, shall I compare thine eyne?
Crystal is muddy: O how ripe in show
Thy lips, those kissing cherries, tempting grow!
That pure congealed white, high Taurus' snow,
145   Fanned with the eastern wind, turns to a crow
When thou hold'st up thy hand. O let me kiss
This princess of pure white, this seal of bliss!

Helena   O spite! O hell! I see you all are bent
To set against me for your merriment:
150   If you were civil, and knew courtesy,
You would not do me thus much injury.
Can you not hate me, as I know you do,
But you must join in souls to mock me too?
If you were men, as men you are in show,
155   You would not use a gentle lady so;
To vow, and swear, and superpraise my parts,
When I am sure you hate me with your hearts.
You both are rivals, and love Hermia;
And now both rivals, to mock Helena.
160   A trim exploit, a manly enterprise,
To conjure tears up in a poor maid's eyes
With your derision! None of noble sort
Would so offend a virgin, and extort
A poor soul's patience, all to make you sport.

165 **Lysander**   You are unkind, Demetrius; be not so;
For you love Hermia; this you know I know;
And here with all good will, with all my heart,
In Hermia's love I yield you up my part;
And yours of Helena to me bequeath,
170   Whom I do love, and will do till my death.

Helena   Nor do you now, in my opinion, now you are giving her up.

Lysander   Demetrius loves her, and he doesn't love you.

Demetrius   [*waking up*] Oh Helen! My goddess! Nymph! So perfect! So divine! How can I describe your eyes? Crystal is muddy by comparison. Oh how tempting your ripe, your cherry lips, have grown! The pure snow that caps the peaks of Turkish mountains, fanned by the winds of the east, turns black as a crow when compared with your hand. Oh, let me kiss this regal whiteness, this blissful seal of happiness!

Helena   Oh, cruelty! Oh, torture! I see you are all determined to gang up on me for your amusement! If you were polite, and knew your manners, you wouldn't hurt me like this. Isn't it enough to hate me, as I know you do, without conspiring to mock me, too? If you were the men you seem to be, you wouldn't abuse a gentle lady like this: vowing and swearing your love, and exaggerating my looks, when I'm sure you hate me heartily. You are both rivals, and love Hermia. Now you rival each other to mock Helena. Very clever – very manly! – to bring tears to a poor girl's eyes through your mockery! No gentleman would offend a maiden so, and try a poor soul's patience, just for fun.

Lysander   You are being unfair, Demetrius. Please don't be. You love Hermia; you know I know this. So now, with the best will in the world and with all my heart, I surrender my share in Hermia's love to you. Bequeath yours of Helena to me: I love her, and will do till I die.

Helena   Never did mockers waste more idle breath.

Demetrius   Lysander, keep thy Hermia; I will none.
If e'er I loved her, all that love is gone.
My heart to her but as guest-wise sojourned,
175   And now to Helen is it home returned,
There to remain.

Lysander   Helen, it is not so.

Demetrius   Disparage not the faith thou dost not know,
Lest to thy peril thou aby it dear.
Look where thy love comes; yonder is thy dear.

[*Enter* **Hermia**]

180   **Hermia**   Dark night, that from the eye his function takes,
The ear more quick of apprehension makes;
Wherein it doth impair the seeing sense,
It pays the hearing double recompense.
Thou art not by mine eye, Lysander, found;
185   Mine ear, I thank it, brought me to thy sound.
But why unkindly didst thou leave me so?

Lysander   Why should he stay whom love doth press to go?

Hermia   What love could press Lysander from my side?

Lysander   Lysander's love, that would not let him bide;
190   Fair Helena, who more engilds the night
Than all yon fiery oes and eyes of light.
Why seek'st thou me? Could not this make thee know
The hate I bear thee made me leave thee so?

Hermia   You speak not as you think; it cannot be.

195   **Helena**   Lo, she is one of this confederacy!
Now I perceive they have conjoined, all three,
To fashion this false sport in spite of me.

Helena   You're wasting your time, the two of you!

Demetrius   Lysander, you stick with Hermia. I don't want her. If I ever did love her, all that love is gone now. My heart only paid her a flying visit: now it has returned home to Helena, where it will stay.

Lysander   Helena, it's not true!

Demetrius   Don't belittle a faith you don't understand, or you might pay dearly for it.

[**Hermia** *enters*]

Look – your loved one is here. There's your sweetheart!

Hermia   The darkness of night, that stops the eyes from waking, makes the ear more sensitive; as it takes away sight, it enhances hearing. I didn't find you by looking, Lysander. It's thanks to my hearing that I'm here. Why did you leave me so inconsiderately?

Lysander   When love drives a man to go, why should he stay?

Hermia   Whose love could drive Lysander from my side?

Lysander   My beloved's: she urges me on – the fair Helena, who beautifies the night more than the sparkling stars! Why do you follow me? Don't you realise I left you because I hated you?

Hermia   You don't mean what you're saying. This can't be so!

Helena   There now! She's in league with the others! Now I understand: all three have got together to play this mean game just to spite me. Hermia – how insulting: how

Injurious Hermia, most ungrateful maid!
Have you conspired, have you with these contrived
200 To bait me with this foul derision?
Is all the counsel that we two have shared,
The sisters' vows, the hours that we have spent,
When we have chid the hasty-footed time
For parting us – O, is all forgot?
205 All school-days' friendship, childhood innocence?
We, Hermia, like two artificial gods,
Have with our needles created both one flower,
Both on one sampler, sitting on one cushion,
Both warbling of one song, both in one key;
210 As if our hands, our sides, voices, and minds
Had been incorporate. So we grew together,
Like to a double cherry, seeming parted,
But yet in union in partition,
Two lovely berries, moulded on one stem;
215 So, with two seeming bodies, but one heart;
Two of the first, like coats in heraldry,
Due but to one and crowned with one crest.
And will you rent our ancient love asunder,
To join with men in scorning your poor friend?
220 It is not friendly, 'tis not maidenly.
Our sex, as well as I, may chide you for it,
Though I alone do feel the injury.

Hermia I am amazed at your passionate words;
I scorn you not; it seems that you scorn me.

225 **Helena** Have you not set Lysander, as in scorn,
To follow me, and praise my eyes and face?
And made your other love, Demetrius,
Who even but now did spurn me with his foot,
To call me goddess, nymph, divine and rare,
230 Precious, celestial? Wherefore speaks he this
To her he hates? And wherefore doth Lysander

ungrateful! Are you part of the conspiracy? Have you plotted with them to persecute me with this cruel mockery? Are all the confidences we two have shared, the vows of sisterly love, the hours we've spent together when we've resented passing time because it parted us – are all these forgotten? Our friendship from schooldays and early childhood? Like two gods at their creative work, Hermia, we've worked together as one person at our needlework, creating a single flower on a single tapestry, sharing a single cushion, singing the same song in the same key – as if our hands, our sides, our voices and our minds had been fused together as one. So we grew up together, like a double cherry: apparently separate, but really a whole divided into two parts. Two lovely berries formed on a single stem; sharing one heart, though possessing two individual bodies. We were like a coat of arms on a shield: divided vertically down the middle, but with a common background, united by a single crest crowning the whole. And will you now tear our longstanding love apart, to ally with men in scorning your poor friend? That isn't friendly. It isn't maidenly. Though I'm the only injured party, every woman – not just me – would censure you for it.

Hermia   Your passionate words amaze me. I'm not scorning you. You seem to be scorning me!

Helena   Haven't you set up Lysander to follow me around in mockery, praising my eyes and my looks? And made your other love, Demetrius – who only recently kicked me around – start calling me 'goddess', 'nymph', 'divine and unique', 'precious' and 'heavenly'? Why does he say this to a woman he hates? And why does Lysander reject

Deny your love, so rich within his soul,
And tender me, forsooth, affection,
But by your setting on, by your consent?
235 What though I be not so in grace as you,
So hung upon with love, so fortunate,
But miserable most, to love unloved.
This you should pity rather than despise.

Hermia   I understand not what you mean by this.

240 **Helena**   Ay, do; persever, counterfeit sad looks,
Make mouths upon me when I turn my back,
Wink each at other, hold the sweet jest up;
This sport, well carried, shall be chronicled.
If you have any pity, grace, or manners,
245 You would not make me such an argument.
But fare ye well; 'tis partly my own fault,
Which death or absence soon shall remedy.

Lysander   Stay, gentle Helena, hear my excuse;
My love, my life, my soul, fair Helena!

Helena   O, excellent!

250 **Hermia**   Sweet, do not scorn her so.

Demetrius   If she cannot entreat, I can compel.

Lysander   Thou canst compel no more than she entreat.
Thy threats have no more strength than her weak prayers.
Helen, I love thee, by my life I do;
255 I swear by that which I will lose for thee
To prove him false that says I love thee not.

Demetrius   I say I love thee more than he can do.

Lysander   If thou say so, withdraw and prove it too.

Demetrius   Quick, come.

your love, so precious to him, and offer his to me (for heaven's sake!) if it wasn't at your instigation, and with your consent? And I not half so favoured as you, so smothered in love, so lucky – but most miserable; loving, but not loved in return! This is a case for pity, not contempt.

Hermia   I don't know what you mean by this!

Helena   Oh yes! Carry on – pretend to look serious; make faces behind my back; tip each other the wink and keep up the oh-so-funny joke! Play this game really well and it will go down in history! If you had any pity, compassion or manners you wouldn't do this to me! So goodbye to you. It's partly my own fault, but my death or disappearance will soon put it right.

Lysander   Don't go dear Helena – listen to my reasons! My love, my life, my soul – beautiful Helena!

Helena   Oh, very funny!

Hermia   [*to* **Lysander**] Dearest, don't mock her like that.

Demetrius   If she can't persuade him, I'll make him!

Lysander   You can't make me, any more than she can persuade. Your threats have no more influence than her weak pleas. Helen, I love you: upon my life I do. I swear by the very life I'd lose for you to fight any man who says I don't love you.

Demetrius   [*to* **Helena**] I say I love you more than he does!

Lysander   Do you? – Then come outside and prove it!

Demetrius   [*making to go*] Come on then, quick . . . .

Hermia   Lysander, whereto tends all
this?

Lysander   Away, you Ethiope.

260 **Demetrius**   No, no; he'll
Seem to break loose; take on as you would follow,
But yet come not; you are a tame man, go!

Lysander   [*struggling with* **Hermia**] Hang off, thou cat,
thou burr; vile thing, let loose,
265   Or I will shake thee from me like a serpent!

Hermia   Why are you grown so rude? What change is this,
Sweet love?

Lysander   Thy love? out, tawny Tartar, out!
Out, loathed medicine; hated potion, hence!

Hermia   Do you not jest?

Helena   Yes, sooth, and so do you.

270 **Lysander**   Demetrius, I will keep my word with thee.

Demetrius   I would I had your bond; for I perceive
A weak bond holds you; I'll not trust your word.

Lysander   What, should I hurt her, strike her, kill her
dead?
275   Although I hate her, I'll not harm her so.

Hermia   What, can you do me greater harm than hate?
Hate me? Wherefore? O me, what news, my love!
Am I not Hermia? Are not you Lysander?
I am as fair now as I was erewhile.
280   Since night you loved me; yet since night you left me.
Why then, you left me – O, the gods forbid! –
In earnest, shall I say?

Hermia   [*holding him back*] Lysander, how's this going to end?

Lysander   [*struggling to escape*] Get off, you blackhead!

Demetrius   Oh yes! Pretend to get away. Act as if you'd like to follow – but stay put! You're a coward. Pah!

Lysander   [*unable to disentangle himself*] Let go, you cat's-claw! You burr! You vile object, take your hands off me, or I'll shake you off like a snake!

Hermia   Why have you turned so nasty? Why the change, sweet love?

Lysander   *Your* love? Off, you swarthy savage, off! Get off, you nasty dose of horrible medicine – away with you!

Hermia   [*holding tight*] You're joking, surely?

Helena   [*still convinced they are pretending*] Yes indeed – and so are you!

Lysander   Demetrius, my challenge still stands!

Demetrius   I wish it was backed by a guarantee! [*mocking* **Hermia's** *grasp*] You don't seem very strongly bonded! You can't be trusted.

Lysander   What – do you want me to hurt her, strike her, or kill her dead? Although I hate her, I can't harm her like that.

Hermia   What? Do you think you can do me greater harm than hating me? Hate me? But why? What's changed things? Aren't I Hermia? Aren't you Lysander? I'm as beautiful now as I ever was. You loved me before this night began, yet you left me during it. So when you left me asleep – Oh, god forbid! Do I take it you were in earnest?

Lysander   Ay, by my life:
And never did desire to see thee more.
Therefore be out of hope, of question, of doubt;
285   Be certain, nothing truer, 'tis no jest
That I do hate thee, and love Helena.

Hermia   O me! you juggler, you canker-blossom,
You thief of love! What, have you come by night
And stolen my love's heart from him?

Helena   Fine, i'faith!
290   Have you no modesty, no maiden shame,
No touch of bashfulness? What, will you tear
Impatient answers from my gentle tongue?
Fie, fie, you counterfeit, you puppet, you!

Hermia   Puppet? why so! Ay, that way goes the game.
295   Now I perceive that she hath made compare
Between our statures; she hath urged her height,
And with her personage, her tall personage,
Her height, forsooth, she hath prevailed with him.
And are you grown so high in his esteem
300   Because I am so dwarfish and so low?
How low am I, thou painted maypole? Speak,
How low am I? I am not yet so low
But that my nails can reach unto thine eyes.

Helena   I pray you, though you mock me, gentlemen,
305   Let her not hurt me. I was never curst;
I have no gift at all in shrewishness;
I am a right maid for my cowardice;
Let her not strike me: you perhaps may think,
Because she is something lower than myself,
That I can match her.

310 **Hermia**   'Lower'! hark, again!

Lysander   Yes, upon my life. And I never wanted to see you again. So abandon hope. There's no argument, no shadow of doubt; be assured, nothing could be more certain! I'm not joking: I hate you and love Helena!

Hermia   Poor me! [*to* **Helena**] You cheat, you fake, you love-thief! What, have you stolen my loved one's heart under cover of night?

Helena   That's rich! Have you no modesty, no maidenly blushes, no touch of bashfulness? What, provoking my gentle tongue to answer roughly back? Shame on you, you sham! You puppet, you!

Hermia   'Puppet'? Oh yes? Oh, so that's your game! [**Hermia** *is much smaller than* **Helena**] Now she's comparing our heights! She's boasting how tall she is! And with her stature, her tall stature – her height, no less! – she's won him over. Have you grown so high in his esteem because I'm so dwarfish, and so small? How small am I? I'm not so small that my nails can't reach your eyes!

[**Lysander** *and* **Demetrius** *hold her back*]

Helena   [*frightened now*] Please, gentlemen – mock me though you do – don't let her hurt me! I've never had a sharp tongue. I'm no shrew. I'm a typical cowardly female. Don't let her hit me. You probably think I'm her match because she's smaller than I am.

Hermia   [*increasing her struggles*] 'Smaller'? Did you hear that, again?

115

Helena   Good Hermia, do not be so bitter with me.
    I evermore did love you, Hermia,
    Did ever keep your counsels, never wronged you;
    Save that, in love unto Demetrius,
315   I told him of your stealth unto this wood.
    He followed you; for love I followed him;
    But he hath chid me hence and threatened me
    To strike me, spurn me, nay to kill me too.
    And now, so you will let me quiet go,
320   To Athens will I bear my folly back,
    And follow you no further. Let me go.
    You see how simple and how fond I am.

Hermia   Why, get you gone! who is't that hinders you?

Helena   A foolish heart, that I leave here behind.

Hermia   What, with Lysander?

325 **Helena**   With Demetrius.

Lysander   Be not afraid, she shall not harm thee, Helena.

Demetrius   No, sir, she shall not, though you take her
    part.

Helena   O, when she's angry, she is keen and shrewd.
330   She was a vixen when she went to school;
    And though she be but little, she is fierce.

Hermia   Little again? nothing but low and little?
    Why will you suffer her to flout me thus?
    Let me come to her.

Lysander   Get you gone, you dwarf,
335   You minimus, of hindering knot-grass made,
    You bead, you acorn.

Demetrius   You are too officious
    In her behalf that scorns your services.

Helena   Good Hermia, don't be so bitter with me. I've
always loved you, Hermia. Always kept your secrets.
Never done you wrong, except that out of love for
Demetrius, I told him of your secret flight into this wood.
He followed you. Out of love, I followed him. He has
scolded me, and threatened to strike me, spurn
me – even kill me, too! And now, if you'll let me slip
away, I'll take my foolish love back to Athens, and follow
you no more. Let me go. You see how naive and loving I
am.

Hermia   Well, go then! What's stopping you?

Helena   A foolish heart that I'm leaving behind here.

Hermia   What – with Lysander?

Helena   With Demetrius.

Lysander   Don't be afraid. She won't hurt you, Helena.

Demetrius   No, sir – she won't – even though you are on
her side.

Helena   Oh, when she's angry, she's sharp-tongued and
malicious. She was a vixen when she was at school.
Though she's little, she's fierce.

Hermia   'Little' again? Nothing but 'small' and 'little'? Why
do you let her insult me like this? Let me get at her!

Lysander   Be off with you, you dwarf! You midget, made of
tangle-weed! You bead! You acorn!

Demetrius   [*to* **Lysander**] You're interfering where you
aren't wanted: she scorns your services. Leave her

117

Let her alone; speak not of Helena;
Take not her part. For if thou dost intend
340   Never so little show of love to her,
Thou shalt aby it.

Lysander   Now she holds me not.
Now follow, if thou dar'st, to try whose right,
Of thine or mine, is most in Helena.

Demetrius   Follow? Nay, I'll go with thee cheek by jowl.

[*Exeunt* **Lysander** *and* **Demetrius**]

345 **Hermia**   You, mistress, all this coil is 'long of you.
Nay, go not back.

Helena   I will not trust you, I,
Nor longer stay in your curst company.
Your hands than mine are quicker for a fray,
My legs are longer, though, to run away.

[*Exit*]

350 **Hermia**   I am amazed, and know not what to say.

[*Exit*]

[**Oberon** *and* **Puck** *come forward*]

Oberon   This is thy negligence; still thou mistak'st;
Or else committ'st thy knaveries wilfully.

Puck   Believe me, king of shadows, I mistook.
Did not you tell me I should know the man
355   By the Athenian garments he had on?
And so far blameless proves my enterprise
That I have 'nointed an Athenian's eyes;

alone. Don't talk about Helena, and don't presume to speak on her behalf, because however little you intend to show your love for her, you'll regret it.

Lysander   She's not holding me back now. So follow me, if you dare, and we'll see who has the greatest right to Helena.

Demetrius   Follow? No – I'll go with you side by side!

[**Lysander** *and* **Demetrius** *leave, hands on swords*]

Hermia   You, madam – all this fuss is over you! [**Helena** *backs off*] No, don't go!

Helena   I can't trust you, I can't. And I won't stay here in your cursed company any longer. Your hands are quicker than mine for a fight, but my legs are longer, though, to run away.

[*She runs off*]

Hermia   I'm astonished. I don't know what to say.

[**Hermia** *follows after*]

[**Oberon** *and* **Puck** *come forward*]

Oberon   This is your fault. Mistakes again – or else you're up to your roguish tricks on purpose.

Puck   Believe me, king of spirits, I made an error. Didn't you tell me I'd know the man by the Athenian clothing he had on? So I'm not guilty in that I *have* anointed an Athenian's eyes. And I'm glad it turned out as it did. I

And so far am I glad it so did sort,
As this their jangling I esteem a sport.

360 **Oberon**   Thou seest these lovers seek a place to fight.
Hie, therefore, Robin, overcast the night;
The starry welkin cover thou anon
With drooping fog as black as Acheron;
And lead these testy rivals so astray
365   As one come not within another's way.
Like to Lysander sometime frame thy tongue,
Then stir Demetrius up with bitter wrong;
And sometime rail thou like Demetrius;
And from each other look thou lead them thus,
370   Till o'er their brows death-counterfeiting sleep
With leaden legs and batty wings doth creep;
Then crush this herb into Lysander's eye;
Whose liquor hath this virtuous property,
To take from thence all error with his might
375   And make his eyeballs roll with wonted sight.
When they next wake, all this derision
Shall seem a dream, and fruitless vision;
And back to Athens shall the lovers wend,
With league whose date till death shall never end.
380   Whiles I in this affair do thee employ,
I'll to my Queen, and beg her Indian boy;
And then I will her charmed eye release
From monster's view, and all things shall be peace.

Puck   My fairy lord, this must be done with haste,
385   For night's swift dragons cut the clouds full fast,
And yonder shines Aurora's harbinger;
At whose approach, ghosts wandering here and there,
Troop home to churchyards. Damned spirits all,
That in crossways and floods have burial,
390   Already to their wormy beds are gone;
For fear lest day should look their shames upon,

think their quarrelling is great fun.

Oberon   You can see that these lovers are looking for a
place to fight. Go, therefore, Robin, and cloud the night.
Cover the sky with low-lying fog, as black as a river in
Hell, and lead these irate rivals so astray that they never
encounter each other. Speak sometimes in Lysander's
voice, and provoke Demetrius with hurtful remarks.
Then, sometimes rant like Demetrius. And that way, see
you keep them apart till death-like sleep on leaden legs
and flitting bat-like wings creeps over their eyes. Then
crush this herb into Lysander's eyes. [*He hands* **Puck** *a
phial*] The liquid has this special power: it has the
potency to remove all errors and make him see as he did
formerly. When he next wakes all this mockery will seem
like a dream, without significance. Thus the lovers will
return to Athens in a friendship that will last throughout
their lives. And while I have you working on this affair,
I'll go to my Queen and beg the Indian boy from her.
Then I'll set her free from the spell that binds her to the
monster, and all will then be peace.

Puck   My fair lord, this must be done quickly. Night is
swiftly passing from the cloudy sky. The morning star
announces the approach of sunrise, the time when
ghosts, wandering here and there, troop home to
churchyards. The spirits of the damned, who are buried
at crossroads, or who lie in the rivers in which they
drowned, have already returned to their wormy graves,
fearful of their shame's exposure to the day. They

They wilfully themselves exile from light,
And must for aye consort with black-browed night.

Oberon But we are spirits of another sort:
395 I with the morning's love have oft made sport,
And, like a forester, the groves may tread
Even till the eastern gate, all fiery red
Opening on Neptune, with fair blessed beams
Turns into yellow gold his salt green streams.
400 But notwithstanding, haste, make no delay:
We may effect this business yet ere day.

[*Exit* **Oberon**]

Puck Up and down, up and down,
I will lead them up and down;
I am feared in field and town;
405 Goblin, lead them up and down.
Here comes one.

[*Enter* **Lysander**]

Lysander Where art thou, proud Demetrius? Speak thou
now.

Puck Here, villain! drawn and ready.
410 Where art thou?

Lysander I will be with thee straight.

Puck   Follow me, then,
To plainer ground.

[*Exit* **Lysander** *as following the voice*]

[*Re-enter* **Demetrius**]

deliberately cut themselves off from daylight and so must
confine themselves to sombre night for all eternity.

Oberon   But we are spirits of a very different sort. I've
often flirted with the goddess of sunrise, and I can walk
through the woods like any forester – even till the fiery-
red beams of the rising sun appear in the east, and turn
the salt-green sea into a yellow gold. But nonetheless, be
quick. Waste no time. We could complete this business
before the start of day.

[**Oberon** *goes*]

Puck   Up and down, up and down,
I will lead them up and down;
I am feared in field and town;
Goblin – lead them up and down.
Here comes one.

[**Lysander** *enters*]

Lysander   Where are you, arrogant Demetrius? Say
something, will you?

Puck   [*in the voice of* **Demetrius**] Here, villain, with my
sword drawn and ready. Where are you?

Lysander   I'll be with you right away.

Puck   Follow me then, to flatter ground.

[**Lysander** *follows the voice and leaves;* **Demetrius** *enters*]

Demetrius   Lysander! speak again:
Thou runaway, thou coward, art thou fled?
415   Speak! In some bush? Where dost thou hide thy head?

Puck   [*As* **Demetrius**] Thou coward, art thou bragging to
the stars,
Telling the bushes that thou look'st for wars,
And wilt not come? Come, recreant, come, thou child;
420   I'll whip thee with a rod. He is defiled
That draws a sword on thee.

Demetrius   Yea, art thou there?

Puck   [*as* **Lysander**] Follow my voice; we'll try no manhood
here.

[*Exeunt*]

[*Re-enter* **Lysander**]

Lysander   He goes before me, and still dares me on;
425   When I come where he calls, then he is gone.
The villain is much lighter-heeled than I:
I followed fast, but faster he did fly,
That fallen am I in dark uneven way,
And here will rest me.

                              Come, thou gentle day;
430   For if but once thou show me thy grey light,
I'll find Demetrius, and revenge this spite.

[*Lies down and sleeps*]

[*Re-enter* **Puck** *and* **Demetrius**]

Demetrius   Lysander: speak again! You runaway! You coward! Have you disappeared? Speak! [*He pokes around with his sword*] In some bush? Where are you hiding yourself?

Puck   [*speaking like* **Lysander**] You coward! Are you bragging to the stars? Telling the bushes how you're looking for a fight? But won't come? Come on, chicken! Come on, little boy! I'll thrash you with a cane – it would be indecent to draw a sword on you!

Demetrius   Oh yes? You're there are you?

Puck   Follow my voice. We won't fight it out here.

[*They go*]

[*Re-enter* **Lysander**]

Lysander   He keeps ahead of me, and continues to dare me on. When I go where he calls, he's gone! The villain is much more nimble-footed than I am. I followed him fast, but he ran faster and now I find myself on dark and bumpy ground. I'll rest here. Come, gentle day – [*He lies down*] just as soon as it's dawn, I'll find Demetrius and revenge this insult.

[*He sleeps*]

[**Puck** *and* **Demetrius** *enter*]

Puck [*as* **Lysander**] Ho, ho, ho! coward, why com'st thou
not?

Demetrius Abide me, if thou dar'st; for well I wot,
435   Thou runn'st before me, shifting every place,
And dar'st not stand, nor look me in the face.
Where art thou now?

Puck [*as* **Lysander**] Come hither, I am here.

Demetrius Nay, then, thou mock'st me; thou shalt buy
440   this dear,
If ever I thy face by daylight see.
Now, go thy way: faintness constraineth me
To measure out my length on this cold bed:
By day's approach look to be visited.

[*Lies down and sleeps*]

[*Enter* **Helena**]

445 **Helena** O weary night, O long and tedious night,
Abate thy hours, shine comforts from the east,
That I may back to Athens by daylight,
From these that my poor company detest;
And sleep, that sometimes shuts up sorrow's eye,
450   Steal me awhile from mine own company.

[*Lies down and sleeps*]

Puck Yet but three? Come one more.
Two of both kinds makes up four.
Here she comes, curst and sad;
Cupid is a knavish lad,
455   Thus to make poor females mad.

[*Enter* **Hermia**]

Puck   [*speaking like* **Lysander**] Oh ho! Coward! Why don't you come?

Demetrius   Wait for me, if you dare. I know very well that you're running ahead of me, and shifting around, and that you daren't stand your ground, nor look me in the face. Where are you now?

Puck   This way! I'm here!

Demetrius   Right then. You're mocking me. You'll pay for this, if I ever see your face in daylight. Carry on then. Weariness compels me to stretch out on this cold ground. Be sure I'll catch up with you when daylight comes.

[*He lies down and sleeps*]

[**Helena** *enters*]

Helena   Such a weary night! What a long and tedious night! Make yourself shorter! Comfort me with sunrise in the east, so I can return to Athens by daylight, away from these people who dislike my poor company. May sleep that can bring respite from sorrow release me from myself for a while.

[*She lies down and sleeps*]

Puck   Still only three? Come one more.
Two of both kinds makes up four.
Here she comes, angry and sad –
Cupid is a knavish lad
Thus to make poor females mad!

[*Enter* **Hermia**]

Hermia   Never so weary, never so in woe,
   Bedabbled with the dew, and torn with briars,
   I can no further crawl, no further go;
   My legs can keep no pace with my desires.
460 Here will I rest me till the break of day.
   Heavens shield Lysander, if they mean a fray!

           [Lies down and sleeps]

Puck   On the ground
   Sleep sound;
   I'll apply
465 To your eye
   Gentle lover, remedy.

[Squeezes the juice on **Lysander's** *eyes]*

   When thou wak'st,
   Thou tak'st
   True delight
470 In the sight
  Of thy former lady's eye;
 And the country proverb known,
 That every man should take his own,
 In your waking shall be shown:
475   Jack shall have Jill,
   Nought shall go ill;

The man shall have his mare again, and all shall be well.

              [Exit]

Hermia   I've never been so weary, never so sad. Wet with
dew, torn with briars, I can't crawl any further, go any
further. I'd like to, but my legs won't let me. I'll rest here
till daybreak. May the heavens protect Lysander, if they
mean to fight!

[*She lies down and sleeps*]

Puck   On the ground
Sleep sound.
I'll apply
To your eye
Gentle lover, remedy.

[*He squeezes the juice on* **Lysander's** *eyes*]

When you wake
You'll take
True delight
In the sight
Of your former lady's eye.
And the country proverb known
That 'every man should take his own'
In your waking shall be shown.
Jack shall have Jill
Nought shall go ill.
'The man shall have his mare again', and all will be well.

[*He goes*]

[*The lovers lie asleep*]

Act four

Scene 1

*The same place. Enter **Titania** and **Bottom**, with the fairies attending, and **Oberon** behind, unseen.*

Titania   Come, sit thee down upon this flowery bed,
While I thy amiable cheeks do coy,
And stick musk-roses in thy sleek smooth head,
And kiss thy fair large ears, my gentle joy.

5 **Bottom** Where's Peaseblossom?

Peaseblossom Ready.

Bottom Scratch my head, Peaseblossom. Where's Monsieur Cobweb?

Cobweb Ready.

10 **Bottom** Monsieur Cobweb, good monsieur, get you your weapons in your hand, and kill me a red-hipped humble-bee on the top of a thistle; and good monsieur, bring me the honey-bag. Do not fret yourself too much in the action, monsieur; and good monsieur, have a care the
15 honey-bag break not; I would be loth to have you overflown with a honey-bag, signior. Where's Monsieur Mustardseed?

Mustardseed Ready.

Bottom Give me your neaf, Monsieur Mustardseed. Pray
20 you, leave your curtsy, good monsieur.

Mustardseed What's your will?

Act four

Scene 1

The wood. *Enter* **Titania** *and* **Bottom**, *with the attendant fairies.* **Oberon** *follows them, unseen.*

Titania Come, sit you down upon this flowery bed, while I caress your lovely cheeks, and put musk-roses in your sleek, smooth head, and kiss your beautiful large ears, my gentle joy.

Bottom Where's Peaseblossom?

Peaseblossom Ready.

Bottom Scratch my head, Peaseblossom. Where's Mister Cobweb?

Cobweb Ready.

Bottom Mister Cobweb, good sir, get your weapons in your hand and kill a red-hipped bumble-bee for me on the top of a thistle. And, good sir, bring me the honeycomb. Don't go to too much trouble doing it, sir. And, good sir, be careful not to damage the honeycomb. I wouldn't like you to be swamped by a honeycomb, signior. Where's Mister Mustardseed?

Mustardseed Ready.

Bottom Shake hands, Mister Mustardseed. [**Mustardseed** *bows*] Now really, there's no need to curtsy, dear sir.

Mustardseed What can I do for you?

Bottom   Nothing, good monsieur, but to help Cavalery
Cobweb to scratch. I must to the barber's, monsieur, for
methinks I am marvellous hairy about the face. And I am
25   such a tender ass, if my hair do but tickle me, I must
scratch.

Titania   What, wilt thou hear some music, my sweet love?

Bottom   I have a reasonable good ear in music. Let's have
the tongs and the bones.

30 **Titania**   Or say, sweet love, what thou desirest to eat.

Bottom   Truly, a peck of provender; I could munch your
good dry oats. Methinks I have a great desire to a bottle of
hay: good hay, sweet hay, hath no fellow.

Titania   I have a venturous fairy, that shall seek
35   The squirrel's hoard, and fetch thee thence new nuts.

Bottom   I had rather have a handful or two of dried peas.
But I pray you, let none of your people stir me; I have an
exposition of sleep come upon me.

Titania   Sleep thou, and I will wind thee in my arms.
40   Fairies, be gone, and be all ways away.

[*Exeunt* **Fairies**]

So doth the woodbine the sweet honeysuckle
Gently entwist; the female ivy so
Enrings the barky fingers of the elm.
O, how I love thee! How I dote on thee!

[*They sleep*]

[*Enter* **Puck**]

Bottom   Nothing, good sir, but to help Captain Cobweb to scratch. [*He feels his chin*] I must go to the barber's, sir. I believe I'm incredibly hairy round the face. I'm such a tender ass, that if my hair tickles me, I've got to scratch.

Titania   Would you like to hear some music, my sweet love?

Bottom   I've a reasonably good musical ear. Let's have triangles and clappers!

Titania   Or say, sweet love, what you'd like to eat?

Bottom   Actually, a large helping of fodder. I could munch some good dry oats. D'y'know, I've got a yearning for a bundle of hay. Good hay, sweet hay, there's nothing like it.

Titania   I have a fairy scout who'll find a squirrel's hoard and bring you some fresh nuts.

Bottom   I'd prefer a handful or two of dried peas. But I'd be grateful if none of your people disturbed me. I've a great yawning for some sleep.

Titania   Then sleep, and I will hold you in my arms. Fairies – go your various ways.

[*The* **Fairies** *leave*]

[*Putting her arms round* **Bottom** *amorously*] This is how the woodbine twists around the honeysuckle, and the ivy round the barky branches of the elm. Oh, how I love you! How I dote on you!

[*They sleep*]

[**Puck** *enters, and meets* **Oberon**]

45 **Oberon**   [*coming forward*] Welcome, good Robin: seest thou
         this sweet sight?
         Her dotage now I do begin to pity;
         For meeting her of late behind the wood,
         Seeking sweet favours for this hateful fool,
50   I did upbraid her, and fall out with her.
         For she his hairy temples then had rounded
         With coronet of fresh and fragrant flowers;
         And that same dew, which sometime on the buds
         Was wont to swell like round and orient pearls,
55   Stood now within the pretty flowerets' eyes,
         Like tears that did their own disgrace bewail.
         When I had at my pleasure taunted her,
         And she in mild terms begged my patience,
         I then did ask of her her changeling child;
60   Which straight she gave me, and her fairy sent
         To bear him to my bower in fairy land.
         And now I have the boy, I will undo
         This hateful imperfection of her eyes.
         And, gentle Puck, take this transformed scalp
65   From off the head of this Athenian swain,
         That he awaking when the other do,
         May all to Athens back again repair,
         And think no more of this night's accidents
         But as the fierce vexation of a dream.
70   But first I will release the fairy queen.

         [*Touches* **Titania's** *eyelids*]

         Be as thou wast wont to be;
         See as thou wast wont to see.
         Dian's bud o'er Cupid's flower
         Hath such force and blessed power.

75   Now my Titania, wake you, my sweet queen.

Oberon Welcome, good Robin. Do you see this sweet sight? I'm beginning to feel sorry for her in her infatuation. When I met her recently behind this copse, where she was looking for garlands for this repulsive idiot, I scolded her, and quarrelled with her, because she'd put a crown of fresh and fragrant flowers round his hairy temples. The dewdrops that used to form like eastern pearls upon the buds, now swelled like tears inside the pretty petals, as if they were lamenting their own disgrace. When I'd had enough of taunting her, and she'd politely begged me to desist, I asked her for the changeling boy. She gave him to me right away, and sent her fairy to escort him to my home in fairyland. Now I've got the boy, I'll remove the spell that has so hatefully distorted her vision. And, gentle Puck, you must remove the ass's head from this Athenian rustic. When he wakes up alongside the others, they can all return to Athens thinking that all the unusual happenings of the night were only the fantasies of a dream. But first, I'll release the fairy queen.

[*He touches* **Titania's** *eyelids with the juice*]

> Be you as you have always been;
> See as you have always seen;
> Chastity will win a heart,
> Better than young Cupid's dart.

Now, Titania, awake, my sweet queen!

[**Titania** *wakes and rises*]

Titania   My Oberon! What visions have I seen!
Methought I was enamoured of an ass.

Oberon   There lies your love.

Titania   How came these things to
pass?
80   O, how mine eyes do loathe his visage now!

Oberon   Silence awhile. Robin, take off this head;
Titania, music call, and strike more dead
Than common sleep, of all these five the sense.

Titania   Music ho, music, such as charmeth sleep!

[*Music plays*]

85 **Puck**   [*To* **Bottom**, *removing ass's head*] Now, when thou
wak'st, with thine own fool's eyes peep.

Oberon   Sound, music; come, my queen, take hands with
me,
And rock the ground whereon these sleepers be.
90   Now thou and I are new in amity,
And will tomorrow midnight solemnly
Dance in Duke Theseus' house triumphantly,
And bless it to all fair prosperity.
There shall the pairs of faithful lovers be
95   Wedded, with Theseus, all in jollity.

Puck   Fairy King, attend and mark;
I do hear the morning lark.

Oberon   Then, my Queen, in silence sad
Trip we after night's shade;
100   We the globe can compass soon,
Swifter than the wandering moon.

Titania   [*waking and rising to her feet*] My Oberon! What
sights I have seen! I thought I was in love with an ass!

Oberon   [*pointing to* **Bottom**] There lies your loved
one . . . .

Titania   How did all this happen? I think he looks repulsive
now.

Oberon   Quiet for a moment. Robin, take off his head.
Titania, summon musicians. [*Turning to* **Bottom** *and the
four lovers*] Put these five into a death-like sleep, deeper
than normal.

Titania   [*calling to her servants*] Music, there, music! The
kind that bewitches sleep!

[*Soft music is played*]

Puck   [*To* **Bottom** *removing the ass's head*] Now, when
you wake, see with your own foolish eyes!

Oberon   Let music sound. Come, my queen, hold hands,
and rock the ground on which these sleepers lie.

[**Oberon** *and* **Titania** *dance*]

Now you and I are friends again. And tomorrow at
midnight, with full ceremony we'll dance in state at
the house of Duke Theseus, and bless it with enduring
prosperity. The pairs of lovers shall be married there, as
will Theseus, with great merrymaking.

Puck   Fairy King, take note and hark.
I can hear the morning lark.

Oberon   Then, my Queen, let's slip away
In silence: Night will soon be day.
Round the world we'll swifter fly
Than the moon up in the sky.

Titania   Come, my lord, and in our flight
Tell me how it came this night
That I sleeping here was found,
105   With these mortals on the ground.

[*Exeunt. The four lovers and* **Bottom** *still lie asleep*]

[*Hunting horns sound. Enter* **Theseus, Hippolyta, Egeus,**
and their train]

Theseus   Go one of you, find out the forester,
For now our observation is performed;
And since we have the vaward of the day,
My love shall hear the music of my hounds.
110   Uncouple in the western valley; let them go;
Dispatch I say, and find the forester.

[*Exit an Attendant*]

We will, fair queen, up to the mountain's top,
And mark the musical confusion
Of hounds and echo in conjunction.

115 **Hippolyta**   I was with Hercules and Cadmus once,
When in a wood of Crete they bayed the bear
With hounds of Sparta; never did I hear
Such gallant chiding; for, besides the groves,
The skies, the fountains, every region near
120   Seemed all one mutual cry. I never heard
So musical a discord, such sweet thunder.

Theseus   My hounds are bred out of the Spartan kind,
So flewed, so sanded, and their heads are hung
With ears that sweep away the morning dew;
125   Crook-kneed and dew-lapped, like Thessalian bulls;
Slow in pursuit, but matched in mouth like bells,

Titania   Come, my lord, and in our flight
Tell me how it was this night
That I sleeping here was found
With these mortals on the ground.

[*They go*]

[**Bottom** *and the four lovers are still asleep. Hunting
horns are heard. Enter* **Theseus, Hippolyta, Egeus** *and
attendants*]

Theseus   One of you go and find the gamekeeper. We've
celebrated May Day, and since it's early morning, my love
shall hear the barking of my hounds. Set the dogs loose
in the western valley! Let them go! [*To* **Attendant**]
Hurry, I tell you. Find the gamekeeper.

[*An* **Attendant** *leaves*]

Fair queen, we'll climb to the top of the mountain and
enjoy the sound of the baying as it re-echoes down
below.

Hippolyta   I was with Hercules and Cadmus once, in a
wood in Crete, where they were bear-hunting with
Spartan hounds. I never heard such courageous barking.
Not only the groves, but the skies, the fountains and the
district round about all seemed to echo in unison. I never
heard anything so musical yet discordant; so thunderous
yet so sweet.

Theseus   My hounds are of the Spartan breed, with the
typical pendulous jowls, and the sandy-coloured coats.
Their long ears trail the ground; they're bow-legged and
with folds of flesh hanging from their throats like bulls
from Thessaly in Greece; slow runners, but matched in

139

Each under each. A cry more tuneable
Was never holla'd to, nor cheered with horn,
In Crete, in Sparta, nor in Thessaly.
130   Judge when you hear. But soft, what nymphs are these?

Egeus   My lord, this is my daughter here asleep,
And this Lysander, this Demetrius is,
This Helena, old Nedar's Helena;
I wonder of their being here together.

135 **Theseus**   No doubt they rose up early to observe
The rite of May; and, hearing our intent,
Came here in grace of our solemnity.
But speak, Egeus; is not this the day
That Hermia should give answer of her choice?

140 **Egeus**   It is, my lord.

Theseus   Go bid the huntsmen wake them with their
horns.

[*Horns sound. A shout within. The lovers wake up*]

Good morrow, friends. Saint Valentine is past:
Begin these wood-birds but to couple now?

Lysander   Pardon, my lord.

[*The lovers kneel*]

145 **Theseus**   I pray you all, stand up.
I know you two are rival enemies.
How comes this gentle concord in the world,
That hatred is so far from jealousy
To sleep by hate, and fear no enmity?

150 **Lysander**   My lord, I shall reply amazedly,

their barking like church bells, each harmonising with the
others – no more musical a cry ever backed the hunters'
calls, nor was cheered on by the hunters' horns, in Crete,
in Sparta or in Thessaly. Judge for yourself when you
hear them. But 'sh! who are these young ladies?

Egeus   My lord, this is my daughter sleeping here; and this
is Lysander; this Demetrius, this Helena – old Nedar's
Helena. I'm surprised they are here together.

Theseus   No doubt they rose early to celebrate May Day,
and hearing of our intentions, came here to honour our
ceremonies. But tell me, Egeus – isn't this the day that
Hermia should announce her intentions?

Egeus   It is, my lord.

Theseus   Go – tell the huntsmen to wake them with their
horns.

[*Hunting horns sound. There are shouts. The lovers wake
up*]

Good morning, my friends. It's long past St Valentine's
Day. Are these wood-birds only beginning to pair off
now?

Lysander   Your pardon, my lord.

[*The lovers kneel*]

Theseus   Be upstanding. [*To* **Demetrius** *and* **Lysander**] I
know you two are rival enemies. How comes this
peaceful harmony into the world, whereby hatred is so
lacking in distrust that those who hate each other sleep
side by side, unafraid of enmity?

Lysander   My lord, I shall reply in puzzlement, half asleep

141

Half sleep, half waking. But as yet, I swear,
I cannot truly say how I came here.
But as I think, for truly would I speak,
And now I do bethink me, so it is:
155 I came with Hermia hither: our intent
Was to be gone from Athens, where we might,
Without the peril of the Athenian law –

Egeus   Enough, enough, my lord; you have enough;
I beg the law, the law, upon his head.
160 They would have stolen away; they would, Demetrius,
Thereby to have defeated you and me:
You of your wife, and me of my consent;
Of my consent, that she should be your wife.

Demetrius   My lord, fair Helen told me of their stealth,
165 Of this their purpose hither to this wood,
And I in fury hither followed them;
Fair Helena in fancy following me.
But, my good lord, I wot not by what power,
But by some power it is, my love to Hermia,
170 Melted as doth the snow, seems to me now
As the remembrance of an idle gaud,
Which in my childhood I did dote upon;
And all the faith, the virtue of my heart,
The object and the pleasure of mine eye,
175 Is only Helena. To her, my lord,
Was I betrothed ere I saw Hermia;
But like in sickness did I loathe this food;
But, as in health, come to my natural taste,
Now I do wish it, love it, long for it,
180 And will for evermore be true to it.

Theseus   Fair lovers, you are fortunately met;
Of this discourse we more will hear anon.
Egeus, I will overbear your will,

and half awake. At the moment, I can't say for sure how I came to be here. I rather think [*he pauses, unsure*] – I want to speak the truth – [*it all comes back*] Now I remember; this is how it is: I came here with Hermia. Our intention was to quit Athens for somewhere where we might, beyond the reach of the laws of Athens –

Egeus   [*cutting him short*] That's enough, enough my lord. You've heard enough! I beg the law – the law! – upon his head. They would have run away. They would, Demetrius! They'd have cheated you and me; you of your wife, and me of my consent, of my permission, that she should be your wife.

Demetrius   My lord, fair Helen told me of their secret flight, and of their reasons for coming to this wood. I followed them here in anger, and fair Helena followed me out of love. But my good lord, I don't know by what power – but some power was involved – my love for Hermia, melted like the snow, now seems like the memory of a futile plaything, which I doted on in my childhood. My whole faith, the life-blood of my heart, the focus and the pleasure of my eye, is solely Helena. To her, my lord, I was engaged before I saw Hermia. In sickness I went off my favourite food; but now restored to health, I've regained my natural taste. Now I wish for it, love it, long for it, and will for evermore be faithful to it.

Theseus   Dear lovers: your meeting together is fortunate. We'll hear more of this story later. Egeus, I will over-rule

For in the temple, by and by, with us
185 These couples shall eternally be knit.
And, for the morning now is something worn,
Our purposed hunting shall be set aside.
Away with us to Athens; three and three,
We'll hold a feast in great solemnity.
190 Come, Hippolyta.

[*Exeunt all but the lovers and* **Bottom,** *still asleep*]

Demetrius   These things seem small and
    undistinguishable,
Like far-off mountains turned into clouds.

Hermia   Methinks I see these things with parted eye,
When everything seems double.

195 **Helena**   So methinks;
And I have found Demetrius, like a jewel,
Mine own, and not mine own.

Demetrius   Are you sure
That we are awake? It seems to me
That yet we sleep, we dream. Do not you think
200 The Duke was here, and bid us follow him?

Hermia   Yea, and my father.

Helena   And Hippolyta.

Lysander   And he did bid us follow to the temple.

Demetrius   Why then, we are awake; let's follow him,
And by the way let us recount our dreams.

[*Exeunt the lovers*]

Bottom   [*Waking up*] When my cue comes, call me, and I

your wishes. In the temple these couples shall be married soon, with us. And because it's now late in the morning, we'll cancel the hunt we had proposed. Let's all return to Athens: all three couples. We'll hold a great ceremonial feast. Come, Hippolyta.

[*Everyone goes but the lovers and* **Bottom**, *who is still asleep*]

Demetrius Everything seems vague and ill-defined: like mountains so distant they look like clouds.

Hermia I think I'm seeing things out of focus. Everything looks double.

Helena Me too. Demetrius is like a jewel I have found: he's mine, but not really mine.

Demetrius Are you sure we are awake? It seems to me we're still asleep, we're dreaming. Didn't you think the Duke was here, and that he told us to follow him?

Hermia Yes, and my father.

Helena And Hippolyta.

Lysander And he told us to follow him to the temple.

Demetrius Well, then, we *are* awake! Let's follow him, and on the way let's describe our dreams.

[*The lovers leave*]

Bottom [*waking up*] When my cue comes, call me and I'll

205   will answer. My next is 'Most fair Pyramus'. Heigh-ho!
       Peter Quince! Flute the bellows-mender! Snout the tinker!
       Starveling! God's my life! Stolen hence, and left me
       asleep! I have had a most rare vision. I have had a dream,
       past the wit of man to say what dream it was. Man is but
210   an ass if he go about to expound this dream. Methought I
       was – there is no man can tell what. Methought I was,
       and methought I had – but man is but a patched fool, if
       he will offer to say what methought I had. The eye of man
       hath not heard, the ear of man hath not seen, man's hand
215   is not able to taste, his tongue to conceive, nor his heart to
       report, what my dream was. I will get Peter Quince to
       write a ballad of this dream; it shall be called 'Bottom's
       Dream', because it hath no bottom; and I will sing it in the
       latter end of the play, before the Duke. Peradventure, to
220   make it the more gracious, I shall sing it at her death.

                                                        [*Exit*]

answer. My next one is 'Most fair Pyramus' [*He yawns*]
Heigh-ho! [*calling*] Peter Quince! Flute the bellows-
mender! Snout the tinker! Starveling! God bless me!
They've sneaked off, and left me asleep! I've had a most
wonderful revelation. I've had a dream beyond a man's
ability to say what the dream was. Any man trying to
interpret it would make an ass of himself. I thought I
was – [*he tries but fails to find the words*] – nobody
could say what. [*He tries again*] I thought I was, and I
thought I had – but a man would be a clown to attempt
to describe what I thought I had. Man's eye has never
heard, man's ear has never seen, man's hand has never
tasted, his tongue never conceived, or his heart reported,
what my dream was. I'll get Peter Quince to write a
ballad about this dream. It will be called 'Bottom's Dream'
because it has no bottom, and I'll sing it at the end
of the play in front of the Duke. Perhaps to make it more
pleasing, I'll sing it when Thisbe dies.

[*He goes*]

Scene 2

Athens. Enter **Quince, Flute, Snout,** *and* **Starveling**.

Quince   Have you sent to Bottom's house? Is he come
home yet?

Starveling   He cannot be heard of. Out of doubt he is
transported.

5 **Flute**   If he come not, then the play is marred. It goes not
forward, doth it?

Quince   It is not possible: you have not a man in all Athens
able to discharge Pyramus, but he.

Flute   No; he hath simply the best wit of any handicraft
10   man in Athens.

Quince   Yea, and the best person too; and he is a very
paramour for a sweet voice.

Flute   You must say 'paragon'. A paramour is, God bless
us, a thing of nought.

[*Enter* **Snug**]

15 **Snug**   Masters! the Duke is coming from the temple, and
there is two or three lords and ladies more married. If our
sport had gone forward, we had all been made men.

Flute   O sweet bully Bottom! Thus hath he lost sixpence a
day during his life; he could not have 'scaped sixpence a
20   day. An the Duke had not given him sixpence a day for
playing Pyramus, I'll be hanged. He would have deserved
it: sixpence a day in Pyramus, or nothing.

[*Enter* **Bottom**]

Scene 2

Athens. Enter **Quince, Flute, Snout,** *and* **Starveling.**

Quince   Have you enquired at Bottom's house? Has he come home yet?

Starveling   There's no sign of him. Without a doubt, he's been carried off.

Flute   If he doesn't turn up, then the play's ruined. It will be cancelled, won't it?

Quince   We couldn't do it. There isn't another man in Athens capable of playing Pyramus but him.

Flute   No. He's simply got more talent than any other Athenian working man.

Quince   Yes, and the best physique, too. As for his sweet voice, he's a paramour.

Flute   You mean 'paragon'. A 'paramour' is, God bless us, a naughty sort of man.

[**Snug** *enters*]

Snug   Gentlemen, the Duke is coming from the temple, and two or three more lords and ladies have been married. If we'd put on our play we'd have made our fortunes.

Flute   Dear brother Bottom! So he's lost a sixpence-a-day pension for the rest of his life! He couldn't miss getting sixpence a day! If the Duke hadn't given him sixpence a day for playing Pyramus, I'll be hanged. He would have deserved it. There was sixpence a day in Pyramus, nothing less.

[**Bottom** *enters*]

Bottom   Where are these lads? Where are these hearts?

Quince   Bottom! O, most courageous day! O, most happy
25   hour!

Bottom   Masters, I am to discourse wonders; but ask me
not what, for if I tell you, I am no true Athenian. I will
tell you everything right as it fell out.

Quince   Let us hear, sweet Bottom.

30 **Bottom**   Not a word of me: all that I will tell you is, that
the Duke hath dined. Get your apparel together, good
strings to your beards, new ribbons to your pumps, meet
presently at the palace; every man look o'er his part; for the
short and the long is, our play is preferred. In any case, let
35   Thisbe have clean linen: and let not him that plays the lion
pare his nails, for they shall hang out for the lion's claws.
And, most dear actors, eat no onions, nor garlic; for we are
to utter sweet breath, and I do not doubt but to hear them
say, it is a sweet comedy. No more words: away, go away!

[*Exeunt*]

Bottom   Where are you, lads? Where are you, me hearties?

Quince   Bottom! What a memorable day! What a happy moment!

Bottom   Gentlemen, I've some amazing things to tell you. But don't ask me what, because if I tell you, I'm no true Athenian. I'll tell you everything just as it happened.

Quince   Let's hear it, Bottom old chap.

Bottom   Mum's the word. All I'll tell you is that the Duke has dined. Get your costumes ready, put strong strings on your false beards, new laces in your shoes, and meet immediately at the palace. Everyone must go over his part, because the long and the short of it is, our play has been chosen. Whatever happens, Thisbe must have clean clothes, and don't let the one who's playing the lion cut his nails, because they must hang out and be the lion's claws. And, dear actors all, don't eat any onions, or garlic. We've got to have sweet smelling breath, then I'm sure they'll say it's a sweet comedy. Say no more: away, go away!

[*They go*]

Act five

Scene 1

Athens. Enter **Theseus, Hippolyta, Philostrate** *and* **Attendants**.

Hippolyta 'Tis strange, my Theseus, that these lovers
    speak of.

Theseus More strange than true. I never may believe
    These antique fables nor these fairy toys.
5   Lovers and madmen have such seething brains,
    Such shaping fantasies, that apprehend
    More than cool reason ever comprehends.
    The lunatic, the lover, and the poet
    Are of imagination all compact.
10   One sees more devils than vast hell can hold;
    This is the madman. The lover, all as frantic,
    Sees Helen's beauty in a brow of Egypt.
    The poet's eye, in a fine frenzy rolling,
    Doth glance from heaven to earth, from earth to heaven,
15   And as imagination bodies forth
    The forms of things unknown, the poet's pen
    Turns them to shapes, and gives to airy nothing
    A local habitation and a name.
    Such tricks hath strong imagination
20   That, if it would but apprehend some joy,
    It comprehends some bringer of that joy.
    Or in the night, imagining some fear,
    How easy is a bush supposed a bear.

Hippolyta But all the story of the night told over,
25   And all their minds transfigured so together,

Act five

Scene 1

Athens. Enter **Theseus, Hippolyta, Philostrate,** *and their* **Attendants.**

Hippolyta   What these lovers tell us is very strange, my Theseus.

Theseus   Too strange to be true. I never can believe these far-fetched stories, or tales about fairies. Lovers and madmen have such inventive minds, such fertile imaginations, that they dream up far more than level heads can ever understand. The lunatic, the lover and the poet are all imaginative. One sees more devils than vast hell could accommodate: that's the madman. The lover, just as demented, sees the beauty of Helen of Troy in a gypsy's swarthy face. The poet's vision – wild with inspiration – ranges from heaven to earth, from earth to heaven, and as his imagination creates new concepts, the poet's pen captures them in words, giving abstract things a concrete reality and identity. Vivid imagination can play such tricks that if it thinks about something delightful, it supposes there must be a supernatural source to it. Likewise at night: imagining there's something to be afraid of, how easy it is to think that a bush is actually a bear!

Hippolyta   The consistency of their story of the night's events, plus the fact that they were all deluded at the

153

More witnesseth than fancy's images,
And grows to something of great constancy;
But howsoever, strange and admirable.

[*Enter* **Lysander**, **Demetrius**, **Hermia** *and* **Helena**]

Theseus   Here come the lovers, full of joy and mirth:
30   Joy, gentle friends, joy and fresh days of love
Accompany your hearts!

Lysander   More than to us,
Wait in your royal walks, your board, your bed!

Theseus   Come now, what masques, what dances shall we
         have
35   To wear away this long age of three hours
Between our after-supper, and bed-time?
Where is our usual manager of mirth?
What revels are in hand? Is there no play
To ease the anguish of a torturing hour?
Call Philostrate.

40 **Philostrate**   Here, mighty Theseus.

Theseus   Say, what abridgement have you for this evening?
What masque? What music? How shall we beguile
The lazy time, if not with some delight?

Philostrate   There is a brief how many sports are ripe:
45   Make choice of which your highness will see first.

Theseus   [*Reads*] 'The battle with the Centaurs, to be sung
By an Athenian eunuch, to the harp'.
We'll none of that. That have I told my love
In glory of my kinsman Hercules.
50   'The riot of the tipsy Bacchanals,
Tearing the Thracian singer in their rage'.
That is an old device, and it was played

same time, suggests there's more to it than mere make-believe. It all adds up to a convincing story, albeit supernatural and astonishing.

[*The lovers enter:* **Lysander, Demetrius, Hermia** *and* **Helena**]

Theseus Here come the lovers, all happiness and high spirits. Happiness, dear friends, happiness and love be in your hearts for evermore!

Lysander May even more of it grace your royal walks, your table, and your bed!

Theseus Well now, what masques or dances shall we have to occupy the three tedious hours between the end of our supper and bed-time? Where is our entertainments manager? What amusements have been arranged? Have we no play to reduce the agony of waiting? Call Philostrate. [*Philostrate steps forward*]

Philostrate Here, mighty Theseus.

Theseus What diversion have you for this evening? What masque? What music? How shall we make slow time pass quickly without some entertainment?

Philostrate Here is a list of the shows that are ready: choose which your highness will see first. [*He hands the* **Duke** *a programme*]

Theseus *The Battle with the Centaurs, to be sung by an Athenian castrato to the accompaniment of the harp?* We'll have none of that! I've told my love all about the feats of my cousin Hercules. *The religious frenzy of the drunken women, tearing Orpheus apart (the singer from Thrace) in their fury.* That's an old one. It was performed

When I from Thebes came last a conqueror.
'The thrice three Muses, mourning for the death
55 Of Learning, late deceased in beggary'.
That is some satire, keen and critical,
Not sorting with a nuptial ceremony.
'A tedious brief scene of young Pyramus
And his love Thisbe; very tragical mirth'.
60 Merry and tragical? Tedious, and brief?
That is hot ice, and wondrous strange snow.
How shall we find the concord of this discord?

Philostrate   A play there is, my lord, some ten words long,
Which is as brief as I have known a play;
65 But by ten words, my lord, it is too long,
Which makes it tedious; for in all the play
There is not one word apt, one player fitted.
And tragical, my noble lord, it is;
For Pyramus therein doth kill himself.
70 Which when I saw rehearsed, I must confess,
Made mine eyes water; but more merry tears,
The passion of loud laughter never shed.

Theseus   What are they that do play it?

Philostrate   Hard-handed men, that work in Athens here,
75 Which never laboured in their minds till now;
And now have toiled their unbreathed memories
With this same play, against your nuptial.

Theseus   And we will hear it.

Philostrate   No, my noble lord,
It is not for you. I have heard it over,
80 And it is nothing, nothing in the world;
Unless you can find sport in their intents,
Extremely stretched and conned with cruel pain,
To do you service.

when I came back from conquering Thebes. *The Nine Muses mourning for the death of Scholarship, which died of neglect*. That's some sharp and critical satire, inappropriate to a wedding ceremony. *A long short play about young Pyramus and his lover Thisbe: very tragical comedy*. Comical tragedy? Long and short? That's like hot ice, and warm snow. How shall we follow the sense of this nonsense?

Philostrate   There's a play, my lord, consisting of ten words, which is as short as I've ever known a play to be. But it's too long by ten words, so it's lengthy: because in the entire play there's not one apt word or one good actor. This one [*he points to the programme*] is certainly tragical, because Pyramus kills himself in it. When I saw it being rehearsed, I must admit it brought tears to my eyes – but never did a fit of loud laughter produce more merry ones!

Theseus   Who's putting it on?

Philostrate   Horny-handed men, workers from Athens here, who never did anything intellectual before, but who've forced their rusty brains to memorise this play to celebrate your wedding.

Theseus   We'll hear it then.

Philostrate   No, my noble lord, it's not for you. I've listened through it all, and it's useless, totally useless – unless you can find amusement in their efforts to do you some service. They've worked hard and memorised their parts with much suffering.

Theseus   I will hear that play.
For never anything can be amiss
85   When simpleness and duty tender it.
Go, bring them in; and take your places, ladies.

[*Exit* **Philostrate**]

Hippolyta   I love not to see wretchedness o'ercharged,
And duty in his service perishing.

Theseus   Why, gentle sweet, you shall see no such thing.

90   **Hippolyta**   He says they can do nothing in this kind.

Theseus   The kinder we, to give them thanks for nothing.
Our sport shall be to take what they mistake;
And what poor duty cannot do, noble respect
Takes it in might, not merit.
95   Where I have come, great clerks have purposed
To greet me with premeditated welcomes;
Where I have seen them shiver and look pale,
Make periods in the midst of sentences,
Throttle their practised accent in their fears,
100   And in conclusion, dumbly have broken off,
Not paying me a welcome. Trust me, sweet,
Out of this silence yet I picked a welcome;
And in the modesty of fearful duty
I read as much as from the rattling tongue
105   Of saucy and audacious eloquence.
Love, therefore, and tongue-tied simplicity,
In least speak most, to my capacity.

[*Enter* **Philostrate**]

Philostrate   So please your grace, the Prologue is
addressed.

Theseus   I'll hear that play. Nothing ever offends that's offered by those who are unsophisticated and dutiful. Go, bring them in. Take your seats, ladies.

[**Philostrate** *bows and leaves*]

Hippolyta   I don't like to see simple wretches overstretching themselves, nor men performing duties that give them pain.

Theseus   Why, my gentle sweetheart, you won't see any such thing.

Hippolyta   He says they have no talent.

Theseus   All the kinder of us to thank them for nothing. Our pleasure will be in taking them seriously when they go wrong. When humble, well-meant efforts fail, good breeding values the intention rather than what's achieved. I've been in situations when learned men have set out to deliver formal speeches of welcome. I've seen them shiver and turn pale, halting in mid-sentence, swallowing the words they've rehearsed in their fear; and finally, they've stopped as if struck dumb, not welcoming me at all. Believe me, sweet: out of that silence I understood a welcome nevertheless; and I valued the simple respect which was shown by that nervous performance as much as the empty words of smart and pushy smooth-talkers. Lovers and tongue-tied simple men speak most when they say least, unless I'm much mistaken.

[**Philostrate** *enters*]

Philostrate   Your grace, an actor is ready to deliver the Prologue.

110 **Theseus**   Let him approach.

[*Trumpets sound*]

[*Enter* **Quince** *as the* **Prologue**]

Quince   If we offend, it is with our good will.
That you should think, we come not to offend,
But with good will. To show our simple skill,
That is the true beginning of our end.
115 Consider then, we come but in despite.
We do not come, as minding to content you,
Our true intent is. All for your delight,
We are not here. That you should here repent you,
The actors are at hand: and by their show,
120 You shall know all, that you are like to know.

Theseus   This fellow doth not stand upon points.

Lysander   He hath rid his prologue like a rough colt: he
knows not the stop. A good moral, my lord: it is not
enough to speak, but to speak true.

125 **Hippolyta**   Indeed he hath played on his prologue like a
child on a recorder, a sound, but not in government.

Theseus   His speech was like a tangled chain: nothing
impaired, but all disordered. Who is next?

[*A trumpet sounds. Enter* **Pyramus**, **Thisbe**, **Wall**,
Moonshine *and* **Lion**]

Theseus   Let him come in.

[*Trumpets sound.* **Quince** *enters in the role of* **Prologue**. *He reads from a scroll, but ignores the punctuation*]

Quince   If we should give offence, it's our intent.
That you should think, we come not to offend,
But only to show our skill. That's what is meant,
That is the real beginning of our end.
Take it therefore, we're here because of spite.
We haven't come intending you to please
Our real aim is. All for your delight
We are not here. That you should have no ease
The actors are at hand; by what they show
You'll know the plot – or all you need to know.

Theseus   [*whispering*] This fellow doesn't worry about punctuation!

Lysander   He's ridden this prologue as if it were an unbroken colt. He hasn't learned how to stop! There's a moral in this, my lord: it's not enough just to speak. One has to speak correctly!

Hippolyta   Indeed – he's played on his prologue like a child on a recorder. He's produced a sound, but it's all confused.

Theseus   His speech was like a tangled chain. Nothing wrong with each part – but everything muddled up. Who's next?

[*A trumpet sounds.* **Bottom** *enters, playing the part of* **Pyramus**; **Flute** *as* **Thisbe**, **Snout** *as* **Wall**, **Starveling** *as* **Moonshine**, *and* **Snug** *as the* **Lion**. *They listen to* **Quince** *speak the* **Prologue**, *and step forward one by one as he introduces them*]

Quince   Gentles, perchance you wonder at this show;
130   But wonder on, till truth make all things plain.
       This man is Pyramus, if you would know;
       This beauteous lady Thisbe is certain.
       This man with lime and rough-cast doth present
       Wall, that vile wall, which did these lovers sunder:
135   And through wall's chink, poor souls, they are content
       To whisper: at the which, let no man wonder.
       This man, with lantern, dog and bush of thorn,
       Presenteth Moonshine; for, if you will know,
       By moonshine did these lovers think no scorn
140   To meet at Ninus' tomb, there, there to woo.
       This grisly beast, which Lion hight by name,
       The trusty Thisbe, coming first by night,
       Did scare away, or rather did affright:
       And as she fled, her mantle she did fall,
145   Which Lion vile with bloody mouth did stain.
       Anon comes Pyramus, sweet youth and tall,
       And finds his trusty Thisbe's mantle slain;
       Whereat with blade, with bloody blameful blade,
       He bravely broached his boiling bloody breast,
150   And Thisbe, tarrying in mulberry shade,
       His dagger drew, and died. For all the rest,
       Let Lion, Moonshine, Wall, and Lovers twain,
       At large discourse, while here they do remain.

                              [*Exeunt all the players but* **Snout**]

Theseus   I wonder if the lion be to speak.

155 **Demetrius**   No wonder, my lord: one lion may, when many
       asses do.

Snout   In this same interlude it doth befall
       That I, one Snout by name, present a wall:
       And such a wall, as I would have you think,

Quince   Gentlefolk. You may wonder why we're here.
  But wonder on, till truth makes all things plain.
  This man is Pyramus, I hope that's clear,
  This lovely lady, Thisbe is her name.
  This man with plaster on him represents
  Wall; the nasty wall which kept the lovers apart;
  And through a hole in it they were content
  To whisper: at which, let no man start.
  This man, with lantern, dog, and thorny bush
  Plays Moonshine. I will tell this fact to you:
  By moonshine had these lovers not a blush
  To meet at Ninus' tomb, and there to woo.
  This grisly beast, who's Lion called by name,
  The faithful Thisbe, arriving first that night,
  Did scare away — or rather, gave a fright:
  And as she fled, a garment she let fall
  Which Lion vile with bloody mouth did stain.
  Soon Pyramus arrives, sweet youth so tall,
  And finds his faithful Thisbe's mantle slain.
  At which, with blade, with bloody blameful blade,
  He bravely pierced his boiling bloody breast;
  And Thisbe, waiting in a mulberry glade,
  His dagger used, and died. For all the rest,
  Let Lion, Moonshine, Wall, and lovers two
  Explain it all as they stay here for you.

[*All the players leave except* **Snout**, *the* **Wall**]

Theseus   I wonder if the lion is going to speak?

Demetrius   It would hardly be surprising, my lord. A lion
  can speak if so many asses can.

Snout   In this same play it does befall
  That I, one Snout by name, will play a wall.
  And such a wall, as I would have you think,

160   That had in it a crannied hole or chink,
Through which the lovers, Pyramus and Thisbe,
Did whisper often, very secretly.
This loam, this rough-cast, and this stone doth show
That I am that same wall; the truth is so.
165   And this the cranny is, right and sinister,
Through which the fearful lovers are to whisper.

Theseus Would you desire lime and hair to speak better?

Demetrius It is the wittiest partition that ever I heard
discourse, my lord.

170 **Theseus** Pyramus draws near the wall; silence.

[*Enter* **Bottom**]

Bottom O grim-looked night, O night with hue so black!
O night, which ever art when day is not!
O night, O night; alack, alack, alack,
I fear my Thisbe's promise is forgot.
175   And thou O wall, O sweet, O lovely wall,
That stand'st between her father's ground and mine,
Thou wall, O wall, O sweet and lovely wall,
Show me thy chink, to blink through with mine eyne.

[**Snout** *holds up his fingers*]

Thanks, courteous wall: Jove shield thee well for this!
180   But what see I? No Thisbe do I see.
O wicked wall, through whom I see no bliss,
Cursed be thy stones for thus deceiving me!

Theseus The wall, methinks, being sensible, should curse
again.

That had in it a cranny, hole, or chink
Through which the lovers Pyramus and Thisbe
Did whisper often, very secretly.
This clay, this rough-cast, and this stone are proof
That I am that same wall, and that's the truth.
And this the cranny is, formed by my finger
Through which the frightened lovers are to whisper.

[*He demonstrates to the audience*]

Theseus   Could lime and horsehair speak better?

Demetrius   It's the most intelligent dividing wall I ever
heard hold forth, my lord!

[**Bottom** *enters as* **Pyramus**]

Theseus   Pyramus approaches the wall. Silence!

Bottom   [*giving it all he has*]
Oh grim-look'd night! Oh night with hue so black!
Oh night, which always is when day is not!
Oh night, oh night, alack, alack, alack,
I fear my Thisbe's promise is forgot!
And you, oh wall, oh sweet, oh lovely wall,
That stands between her father's land and mine,
You wall, oh wall, oh sweet and lovely wall,
Show me your chink, to blink through with my eye

[**Snout** *shapes a chink with his fingers*]

Thanks, courteous wall. Jove guard you well for this!
But what see I? No Thisbe do I see.
Oh, wicked wall, through whom I see no bliss,
Cursed be your stones for thus deceiving me!

Theseus   I think the wall, having intelligence, should swear
back.

185 **Bottom**   No in truth sir, he should not. 'Deceiving me' is
Thisbe's cue; she is to enter now, and I am to spy her
through the wall. You shall see it will fall pat as I told you:
yonder she comes.

[*Enter* **Flute**]

Flute   O wall, full often hast thou heard my moans,
190 For parting my fair Pyramus and me.
My cherry lips have often kissed thy stones;
Thy stones, with lime and hair knit up in thee.

Bottom   I see a voice; now will I to the chink,
To spy an I can hear my Thisbe's face.
195 Thisbe!

Flute   My love! thou art my love, I think.

Bottom   Think what thou wilt, I am thy lover's grace,
And like Limander am I trusty still.

Flute   And I like Helen, till the Fates me kill.

200 **Bottom**   Not Shafalus to Procrus was so true.

Flute   As Shafalus to Procrus, I to you.

Bottom   O kiss me through the hole of this vile wall.

Bottom [*stepping out of the part to explain*] No, really sir,
he shouldn't. 'Deceiving me' is Thisbe's cue. She will
enter now, and I am to spy her through the wall. You'll
see it will happen just as I've told you. Here she comes.

[**Flute** *enters dressed as* **Thisbe**]

Flute Oh wall, you've often heard my moans
For separating Pyramus and me.
My cherry lips have often kissed your stones;
Your stones, with lime and hair bound up in thee.

Bottom [*as* **Pyramus**]
I see a voice. I'll go now to the chink
To see if I can hear my Thisbe's face.
Thisbe!

Flute [*as* **Thisbe**]
My love! You *are* my love, I think?

Bottom [*as* **Pyramus**]
Think what you like, your true love I embrace!
And like Limander I am faithful still.

Flute [*as* **Thisbe**]
And I like Helen, till the Fates me kill.

Bottom [*as* **Pyramus**]
Not Shafalus to Procrus was so true.

Flute [*as* **Thisbe**]
As Shafalus to Procrus, I to you.

Bottom [*as* **Pyramus**]
Oh kiss me through the hole of this vile wall.

[*He puts his lips to* **Wall's** *fingers*]

167

Flute   I kiss the wall's hole, not your lips at all.

Bottom   Wilt thou at Ninny's tomb meet me straightway?

205 **Flute**   'Tide life, 'tide death, I come without delay.

[*Exeunt* **Bottom** *and* **Flute**]

Snout   Thus have I, Wall, my part discharged so;
And being done, thus Wall away doth go.

[*Exit*]

Theseus   Now is the Moon used between the two
neighbours.

210 **Demetrius**   No remedy, my lord, when walls are so wilful,
to hear without warning.

Hippolyta   This is the silliest stuff that ever I heard.

Theseus   The best in this kind are but shadows, and the
worst are no worse, if imagination amend them.

215 **Hippolyta**   It must be your imagination then, and not
theirs.

Theseus   If we imagine no worse of them than they of
themselves, they may pass for excellent men. Here come
two noble beasts in, a man and a lion.

[*Enter* **Snug** *and* **Starveling**]

220 **Snug**   You, ladies, you, whose gentle hearts do fear

Flute   [*as* **Thisbe**]
I kiss the wall's hole, not your lips at all.

Bottom   [*as* **Pyramus**]
Will you at Ninny's tomb meet me straightaway?

Flute   [*as* **Thisbe**]
Come life or death, I'll go without delay.

[**Pyramus** *and* **Thisbe** *leave*]

Snout   [*as* **Wall**]
Thus have I, as the wall, performed my part.
So having done, the Wall can now depart.

[*The* **Wall** *exits*]

Theseus   The moon will now have to come between the two lovers.

Demetrius   There's no alternative, my lord, especially when walls have ears.

Hippolyta   This is the silliest stuff I ever heard!

Theseus   Even the best actors are only shamming, so the worst can't be any worse, if aided by the imagination.

Hippolyta   It must be *your* imagination then, not theirs!

Theseus   If we think no less of them than they do of themselves, they'll pass as excellent men! Here come two noble beasts; a man and a lion.

[**Snug** *enters as* **Lion**, *and* **Starveling** *as* **Moonshine**]

Snug   [*as* **Lion**]
You, ladies, whose gentle hearts do fear

The smallest monstrous mouse that creeps on floor,
May now, perchance, both quake and tremble here
When Lion rough in wildest rage doth roar.
Then know that I, one Snug the joiner, am
225   A lion fell, nor else no lion's dam:
For if I should as Lion come in strife
Into this place, 'twere pity on my life.

Theseus   A very gentle beast, and of a good conscience.

Demetrius   The very best at a beast, my lord, that e'er I
230   saw.

Lysander   This Lion is a very fox for his valour.

Theseus   True, and a goose for his discretion.

Demetrius   Not so, my lord; for his valour cannot carry his
discretion, and the fox carries the goose.

235 **Theseus**   His discretion, I am sure, cannot carry his valour;
for the goose carries not the fox. It is well; leave it to his
discretion, and let us listen to the Moon.

Starveling   This lanthorn doth the horned moon present.

Demetrius   He should have worn the horns on his head.

240 **Theseus**   He is no crescent and his horns are invisible,
within the circumference.

Starveling   This lanthorn doth the horned moon present:
Myself the Man i' th' Moon do seem to be.

Theseus   This is the greatest error of all the rest; the man
245   should be put into the lantern. How is it else the Man i'
th' Moon?

The smallest monstrous mouse that creeps on floor,
May now, perhaps, both quake and tremble here
When Lion rough in wildest rage does roar.
So know that I, one Snug, – in real life
A joiner – am a Lion; not its wife.
If I should enter with a lion's roar
My life would not be worth a single straw.

Theseus   A very gentle beast, with a tender conscience.

Demetrius   The beastliest actor I ever saw, my lord!

Lysander   This lion has all the courage of a fox!

Theseus   True, and as much caution as a goose.

Demetrius   No, my lord, that's not so. His courage can't overcome his caution, but a fox can overcome a goose.

Theseus   His caution can't overcome his courage, of that I'm sure: no goose ever overcomes a fox. All right. Leave it for him to decide which he is, and let's listen to the Moon.

Starveling   [as **Moonshine**] This lantern represents the crescent moon. [*He holds it up for all to see*]

Demetrius   He should have worn it on top of his lead: his wife's such a light woman.

Theseus   [*shaking his head in disagreement*] He isn't big enough, and you can't see how horny he is.

Starveling   [as **Moonshine**] This lantern represents the crescent moon,
And I'm the Man in the moon, so it would seem.

Theseus   This is the greatest error of them all. The man should be inside the lantern. How else can he be the Man in the Moon?

Demetrius   He dares not come there for the candle; for you
see, it is already in snuff.

Hippolyta   I am a-weary of this Moon; would he would
250   change!

Theseus   It appears, by his small light of discretion, that he
is in the wane: but yet, in courtesy, in all reason, we must
stay the time.

Lysander   Proceed, Moon.

255 **Starveling**   All that I have to say is to tell you that the
lantern is the Moon; I, the Man i' th' Moon; this thornbush,
my thornbush; and this dog, my dog.

Demetrius   Why, all these should be in the lantern: for all
these are in the Moon. But silence, here comes Thisbe.

[*Enter* **Flute**]

260 **Flute**   This is old Ninny's tomb. Where is my love?

Snug   Oh-h-h-!

[**Flute** *runs off*]

Demetrius   Well roared, Lion.

Theseus   Well run, Thisbe.

265 **Hippolyta**   Well shone, Moon. Truly the moon shines
with a good grace.

[**Snug** *tears* **Thisbe's** *mantle and exits*]

Theseus   Well moused, Lion.

[*Enter* **Bottom**]

Demetrius   He daren't because of the candle. It's smoking.

Hippolyta   I'm fed up with this Moon. I wish it would change.

Theseus   Judging by his dimness, he's on the wane. But in all fairness and commonsense, we must sit this one out.

Lysander   Proceed, Moon.

Starveling   [*No nonsense*] All I've got to say is to tell you that this lantern is the Moon. I'm the Man in the Moon. This thorn-bush is my thorn-bush. This dog is my dog.

Demetrius   All of these should be inside the lantern, since all these are in the moon. But silence – here comes Thisbe!

[**Flute** *returns, as* **Thisbe**]

Flute   This is old Ninny's Tomb. Where is my love?

Snug   [*as* **Lion**] Roar – r – r – r!

[**Thisbe** *runs away, leaving behind her mantle*]

Demetrius   Well roared, lion!

Theseus   Well run, Thisbe!

Hippolyta   Well shone, Moon! Truly, the moon shines very gracefully.

[**Lion** *worries the fallen mantle vigorously and leaves*]

Theseus   Well moused, Lion!

[**Bottom** *returns as* **Pyramus**]

Demetrius   And then came Pyramus.

Lysander   And so the Lion vanished.

Bottom   Sweet Moon, I thank thee for thy sunny beams;
270   I thank thee, Moon, for shinning now so bright;
For by thy gracious, golden, glittering gleams,
I trust to take of truest Thisbe sight.

But stay! O spite!
But mark, poor knight,
275   What dreadful dole is here?
Eyes, do you see?
How can it be?
O dainty duck! O dear!
Thy mantle good,
280   What! Stained with blood?
Approach, ye furies fell!
O Fates, come come!
Cut thread and thrum:
Quail, crush, conclude, and quell.

285   **Theseus**   This passion, and the death of a dear friend,
would go near to make a man look sad.

Hippolyta   Beshrew my heart, but I pity the man.

Bottom   O wherefore, Nature, didst thou lions frame,
Since lion vile hath here deflowered my dear?
290   Which is – no, no, which was – the fairest dame
That lived, that loved, that liked, that looked with
cheer.

Come tears, confound:
Out sword and wound
295   The pap of Pyramus;

Demetrius Then Pyramus came.

Lysander So the Lion vanished.

Bottom [*In grandest fashion, with elaborate gestures*]

Sweet Moon, I thank you for your sunny beams.
I thank you, Moon, for shining now so bright,
For by your gracious, golden, glittering gleams
I hope of faithful Thisbe to catch sight.

[*He sees the torn mantle on the ground*]

But stay! O spite!
But mark, poor knight,
What dreadful woe is here!
Eyes, do you see?
How can it be?
Oh, dainty duck! Oh dear!
Your mantle good
What, stained with blood?
Approach you Furies fell:
Oh, Fates! Come, come:
Cut thread and thrum.
Quail, crush, conclude and quell!

Theseus [*drily*] This distress, and the death of a dear
friend, would indeed make a man look miserable.

Hippolyta Curse my heart, but I pity the man!

Bottom [*as* **Pyramus**]

Oh wherefore, Nature, did you lions frame?
Since lion vile has here destroyed my dear
Which is – no, no, which was – the fairest dame
That lived, that loved, that liked, that looked with cheer.

Come tears, confound!
Out sword, and wound
The breast of Pyramus.

Ay, that left pap,
Where heart doth hop:
Thus die I, thus, thus, thus!
Now am I dead,
300   Now am I fled;
My soul is in the sky.
Tongue, lose thy light,
Moon, take thy flight!

[Exit **Starveling***]*

Now die, die, die, die, die.

305 **Demetrius**   No die, but an ace for him; for he is but one.

Lysander   Less than an ace, man; for he is dead, he is nothing.

Theseus   With the help of a surgeon he might yet recover, and prove an ass.

310 **Hippolyta**   How chance Moonshine is gone before Thisbe comes back and finds her lover?

[Enter **Flute***]*

Theseus   She will find him by starlight. Here she comes, and her passion ends the play.

Hippolyta   Methinks she should not use a long one for
315 such a Pyramus; I hope she will be brief.

Demetrius   A mote will turn the balance, which Pyramus, which Thisbe is the better; he for a man, God warrant us, she for a woman, God bless us.

Ay, that left teat
Where heart does beat
Thus I die, thus, thus, thus.   [*He stabs himself*]
Now I am dead
Now I am fled
My soul is in the sky.
Tongue, lose your sight
Moon, take your flight!

[**Moonshine** *exits*]

Now die, die, die, die, die.

[*He dies dramatically*]

Demetrius   He's got the lowest score in the dice with
death: one!

Lysander   Less than one, man, because being dead, he's
nothing!

Theseus   With the help of a doctor he might still recover
and be an ass.

Hippolyta   How come Moonshine has gone before Thisbe
comes back and finds her lover?

[**Thisbe** *returns*]

Theseus   She'll find him by the light of the stars. Here she
comes, and her passionate speech will end the play.

Hippolyta   I don't think she should go in for a long one for
a Pyramus such as this. I hope she'll be brief.

Demetrius   It's a fine point as to whether Pyramus or
Thisbe is the better – he as a man, God preserve us, or
she as a woman, God bless us!

Lysander   She hath spied him already with those sweet
320   eyes.

Demetrius   And she moans, videlicet –

Flute   Asleep, my love?
          What, dead, my dove?
     O Pyramus arise!
325   Speak, speak! Quite dumb?
          Dead, dead? A tomb
     Must cover thy sweet eyes.
          These lily lips,
          This cherry nose,
330   These yellow cowslip cheeks,
          Are gone, are gone!
          Lovers, make moan;
     His eyes were green as leeks.
          O Sisters Three,
335   Come, come to me,
     With hands as pale as milk;
          Lay them in gore,
          Since you have shore
     With shears his thread of silk.
340   Tongue, not a word:
          Come, trusty sword,
     Come, blade, my breast imbrue!
          And farewell, friends;
          Thus Thisbe ends:
345   Adieu, adieu, adieu!

Theseus   Moonshine and Lion are left to bury the dead.

Demetrius   Ay, and Wall too.

Lysander   She's noticed him already with those sweet eyes
of hers.

Demetrius   And she grieves; namely –

Flute   [*as* **Thisbe**]
     Asleep, my love?
     What, dead, my dove?
Oh Pyramus, arise!
     Speak, speak. Quite dumb?
     Dead, dead? A tomb
Must cover your sweet eyes.
     These lily lips,
     This cherry nose,
These yellow cowslip cheeks,
     Are gone, are gone;
     Lovers make moan:
His eyes were green as leeks.
     O Sisters Three,
     Come, come to me
With hands as pale as milk;
     Lay them in blood
     And then you could
Cut through his thread of silk.
     Tongue, not a word:
     Come, trusty sword,
Come blade, my breast stab through.   [*She stabs herself*]
     And farewell, friends.
     Thus Thisbe ends –
Adieu, adieu, adieu.

                                    [*She dies*]

Theseus   Moonshine and Lion are left to bury the dead.

Demetrius   Yes, and the Wall too.

Bottom   No, I assure you, the wall is down that parted
their fathers. Will it please you to see the epilogue, or to
350   hear a Bergomask dance between two of our company?

Theseus   No epilogue, I pray you; for your play needs no
excuse. Never excuse; for when the players are all dead
there need none to be blamed. Marry, if he that writ it
had played Pyramus, and hanged himself in Thisbe's
355   garter, it would have been a fine tragedy: and so it is truly,
and very notably discharged. But come, your Bergomask:
let your epilogue alone.

[*A dance*]

The iron tongue of midnight hath told twelve.
Lovers, to bed; 'tis almost fairy time.
360   I fear we shall out-sleep the coming morn
As much as we this night have overwatched.
This palpable gross play hath well beguiled
The heavy gait of night. Sweet friends, to bed.
A fortnight hold we this solemnity,
365   In nightly revels and new jollity.

[*Exeunt all*]

[*Enter* **Puck**]

Puck   Now the hungry lion roars,
And the wolf behowls the moon;
Whilst the heavy ploughman snores,
All with weary task fordone.
370   Now the wasted brands do glow,
Whilst the screech-owl, screeching loud,
Puts the wretch that lies in woe
In remembrance of a shroud.
Now it is the time of night
375   That the graves, all gaping wide,

Bottom   [*rising to his feet*] No, I can assure you. The wall
has been taken down that separated their fathers. Would
you like to see the epilogue, or to hear a rustic dance
between two of our company?

Theseus   Please, no epilogue! Your play needs no apology.
Never apologise, because since the actors are all dead,
no one need be blamed. Indeed, if the author had played
Pyramus, and hanged himself in Thisbe's garter, then it
would have been a very pleasing tragedy. And so it was,
honestly, and performed very notably. But come – your
rustic dance: forget the epilogue.

[*The Athenian men dance a Bergomask Dance*]

The bell has tolled midnight. Lovers: to bed. It's almost
time for the fairies. I'm afraid we'll oversleep tomorrow
morning as much as we've stayed up late tonight. This
utterly awful play has made the time pass quickly. Sweet
friends, to bed. We'll celebrate for a fortnight, with
revelry at night and fresh entertainments.

[*They all go*]

[**Puck** *enters with a sweeping brush*]

Puck   Now the hungry lion roars,
And the wolf howls at the moon;
Whilst the dog-tired ploughman snores,
Weary from the task he's done.
Now the burnt-out logs just glow
Whilst the screech-owl, screeching loud,
Makes the wretch who lies in woe
Think about a funeral shroud.
Now it is the time of night
When all the graves are gaping wide.

Every one lets forth his sprite,
In the church-way paths to glide.
And we fairies, that do run
By the triple Hecate's team
380   From the presence of the sun,
Following darkness like a dream,
Now are frolic; not a mouse
Shall disturb this hallowed house.
I am sent with broom before,
385   To sweep the dust behind the door.

[*Enter* **Oberon** *and* **Titania**, *the king and queen of Fairies,*
with their train]

Oberon   Through the house give glimmering light,
By the dead and drowsy fire;
Every elf and fairy sprite
Hop as light as bird from briar;
390   And this ditty after me
Sing, and dance it trippingly.

Titania   First rehearse your song by rote,
To each word a warbling note.
Hand in hand, with fairy grace,
395   Will we sing and bless this place.

[**Oberon** *leading, the* **Fairies** *sing and dance*]

Oberon   Now until the break of day,
Through this house each fairy stray.
To the best bride-bed will we,
Which by us shall blessed be;
400   And the issue there create
Ever shall be fortunate.

Each lets out a ghostly sprite
In the church-way paths to glide.
And we fairies, who all run
As members of Queen Hecate's team
From the presence of the sun,
Following darkness like a dream,
Now are happy. Not a mouse
Shall disturb this holy house.
I've been sent, broom to the fore,
To sweep the dust behind the door.

[**Oberon** and **Titania**, *king and queen of the Fairies, enter with their train. Each* **Fairy** *is wearing a headband on which is fixed a candle*]

Oberon   [*To the* **Fairies**]

Through the house give glimmering light
Around the dead and drowsy fire.
Every elf and fairy sprite
Hop as light as bird from briar.
And this ditty after me
Sing, and dance it trippingly.

Titania   First repeat your song by rote
Give each word a warbling note.
Hand in hand with fairy grace
We will sing and bless this place.

[**Oberon** *takes the lead in a fairy dance*]

Oberon   Now until the break of day
Through this house each fairy stray.
We'll go to Duke Theseus' bed
Where there'll be a blessing said.
All the children they create
Ever shall be fortunate.

So shall all the couples three
Ever true in loving be;
And the blots of Nature's hand
405   Shall not in their issue stand.
Never mole, hare-lip, nor scar,
Nor mark prodigious, such as are
Despised in nativity,
Shall upon their children be.
410   With this field-dew consecrate,
Every fairy take his gait,
And each several chamber bless,
Through this palace, with sweet peace;
And the owner of it blest
415   Ever shall in safety rest.
Trip away, make no stay;
Meet me all by break of day.

[*Exeunt all but* **Puck**]

Puck   If we shadows have offended,
Think but this, and all is mended,
420   That you have but slumbered here,
While these visions did appear.
And this weak and idle theme,
No more yielding but a dream,
Gentles do not reprehend:
425   If you pardon, we will mend.
And, as I am an honest Puck,
If we have unearned luck
Now to scape the serpent's tongue,
We will make amends ere long;
430   Else the Puck a liar call.
So, good night unto you all.
Give me your hands, if we be friends,
And Robin shall restore amends.

[*Exit*]

So shall all the couples three
Ever true in loving be;
Perfect offspring they'll beget;
Blemishes they can forget:
Not a mole, hare-lip, or scar,
Nor birthmark, flaws which often are
What parents fear, and often mourn,
Shall affect their children born.
With this pure and holy dew
Every fairy this must do:
Each and every chamber bless
Give the palace peacefulness.
With the owner of it blessed,
Ever he'll in safety rest.
Trip away and don't delay;
Meet me all by break of day.

[*They all go except* **Puck**]

Puck   If we actors have offended
Think only this, and all is mended:
That you've only slumbered here
While these visions did appear.
And this weak and pointless theme
Was nothing better than a dream.
Gentle folk do not reprove –
Pardon us, and we'll improve.
And true as I'm an honest Puck,
Should we have the special luck
Not to earn your scornful hiss
We'll soon mend what's now amiss.
Else, the Puck a liar call.
So, good night unto you all!
Clap your hands if we be friends
And Robin will soon make amends.

[*He goes*]

Activities
Characters

Search the text to find answers to the following questions. They will help you to form personal opinions about the characters in the play. Record any relevant quotations *in Shakespeare's own words*.

The nobles

Theseus

1 Theseus appears in the first scene of the play, *Act 1 Scene 1*.

   a From his instructions to Philostrate, what can we deduce about his attitude to life at this time?

   b From his words to Hippolyta, what do we learn of his former activities?

   c From the way Egeus speaks to him what is his status in Athenian society?

   d From his words to Hermia, what do we learn of his

      i views on the duty of children

      ii views on chastity

      iii views on marriage?

   e From his final words in *Act 1 Scene 1* what do we learn of

      i his attitude to Demetrius

      ii his sense of social responsibility

      iii his sensitivity to Hippolyta's feelings?

2 We next see Theseus in *Act 4 Scene 1*

   a Why is he out so early?

b How do we know he is an enthusiastic hunter?

c Is what he says to Egeus consistent with what he has said to Hermia in *Act 1 Scene 1*? What has happened to make him change his attitude?

3 Theseus appears again in the play's final scene, *Act 5 Scene 1*.

    a From his first speech, what do we learn of the Duke's attitude to things of the imagination?

    b How would you describe the kind of man who might hold such attitudes?

    c What information about Theseus is there in *Act 2 Scene 1* that could be quoted as supporting evidence?

4 **a** Theseus's comments on the available entertainments contain clues as to his tastes and personal history. Identify them.

    b His comments on those of lower rank than himself are illuminating. What is his attitude to such people?

    c How would you describe his comments on the play of *Pyramus and Thisbe*?

Hippolyta

1 How can we tell from *Act 1 Scene 1* that Hippolyta has more patience than Theseus?

2 How can we tell from *Act 5 Scene 1* that she is

    a more imaginative

    b more sensitive

    c less willing to suffer fools gladly

    d more easily bored?

Egeus

1 Egeus appears in *Act 1 Scene 1* and *Act 4 Scene 1*. In both scenes he is 'full of vexations'. Explain them.

2 From *Act 1 Scene 1*, identify the lines which show that

Egeus has no understanding of, or sympathy for, romantic love.

3 From what Egeus says in *Act 1 Scene 1*, how do we know that he regards a daughter as a personal possession?

The lovers

Lysander and Demetrius

1 Which of the two has

a a history of inconstancy?
b shown himself to be the more ardent lover?
c given Theseus cause for concern?

2 Which of the two seems (on the whole) to do most

a cursing
b wooing?

3 Which of the two remains under Oberon's spell even at the end of the play?

4 Which of the two pokes most fun at the tradesmen who perform *Pyramus and Thisbe*?

Hermia and Helena

1 **a** Which of the two is short, and which tall?
b Which is dark, and which fair?
c Which of the two is short-tempered, and which the more timid?
d Which of the two is under greatest personal threat?
e Which of the two (on the whole) seems to suffer most?
f Which of the two betrays a confidence?
g Which of the two made her mark at school, and what for?
h Which of the two has been jilted before the play begins?
i Which of the two seems to seek pity?
j Which of the two seems to have the stronger character?

2   A leading Shakespearian critic (R.W. Chambers, in *Man's Unconquerable Mind*) has found Hermia more attractive than Helena. Make out a case for your own personal preference.

The tradesmen

Bottom

1   From his first sentence in *Act 1 Scene 2*, we know Bottom is
   a self-confident and bossy
   b over-ambitious in his use of words.
   Find the evidence, and further examples in the play of these two characteristics.

2   Bottom is a man for all parts.
   a How many does he claim he can play?
   b How often does he change his voice by way of demonstration?

3   Peter Quince persuades Bottom to play Pyramus. What clinches the argument, and why are we amused?

4   When the players meet in the wood to rehearse (*Act 3 Scene 1*), Bottom is immediately in characteristic form.
   a Demonstrate how he has given thought to the production.
   b Show how Bottom creates his own problems, and how he then proceeds to solve them.
   c Illustrate how he has to have the last word.
   Find other examples of his problem-solving.

5   During the rehearsal, Bottom acquires his ass's head, and he converses with the delicate Titania and her fairies.
   a How does he react to her words of flattery?
   b What is his manner with the four attendant fairies?
   Is all this to his credit?

Activities

6 **a** Bottom's supreme moments of being the centre of admiring attention occur in *Act 4 Scene 1*. Find examples of
　　 i his courtesy
　　 ii his vanity.

　b Titania offers refined pleasures; Bottom asks for coarse ones.
　　 i Give examples, and comment on the comic effect.
　　 ii How is the contrast between Bottom and the fairies emphasised by Titania's use of natural things?

7 Bottom wakes up without his ass's head at the end of *Act 4 Scene 1*. He delivers a soliloquy containing many characteristic Bottom-isms.

　a Bottom never likes to be caught off-balance. How do his first words demonstrate this?

　b Bottom is never guilty of modesty. Show how his attempts to describe his dream
　　 i confirm his vanity
　　 ii render him (almost) speechless
　　 iii cause him to embark on a passage of ludicrous eloquence.

　c Finally, Bottom decides that his dream is worthy of permanent record.
　　 i Comment on the proposed title of the commemorative ballad.
　　 ii Comment on the reason for this title
　　 iii Comment on the use to which the ballad will first be put
　　 iv Comment on Bottom's view of its appropriate position in the *Pyramus and Thisbe* play

　—so as to bring out qualities which have led a critic to say that the conclusion of this monologue 'is the finest thing in it'.

8   From the remarks of his fellow-artisans at the beginning of *Act 4 Scene 2*, what do we gather was their unanimous opinion of him

   a as an actor
   b as a singer?
   How are Bottom's words on his return typical of him?

9   Re-read the *Pyramus and Thisbe* interlude in *Act 5 Scene 1*. Find examples of comic absurdity

   a in Bottom's declamatory speeches
   b in his attitude to Wall and Moonshine
   c in his mixing of the senses of perception
   d in stepping out of his part
   e in his use of classical references
   f in his death scene.

10   To Puck, Bottom is 'the shallowest thick-skin' of the 'lumpen homespuns' from Athens. Find examples of the following, and say whether they are redeeming features or further examples of his clownish idiocy:

   a His ability to keep calm
   b His ability to solve problems
   c His self-confidence
   d His lack of self-awareness
   e His qualities of leadership
   f His adaptability.
   Why was Bottom Shakespeare's best choice as the victim of Puck's mischievousness?

Peter Quince, Francis Flute, Tom Snout, Snug and Robin Starveling

1   Although Bottom dominates the scenes in which the tradesmen appear, Shakespeare makes each of his companions distinctive.

a Though Peter Quince lacks Bottom's strength of character, he shows he can be

    i determined when he needs to be

    ii a manager of men by subtle means.

Find examples in *Act 1 Scene 2*.

b Quince also has a talent which Bottom does not attempt to rival. There is a reference to it in *Act 3 Scene 1*, and *Act 4 Scene 1*. What is it?

c Quince corrects Bottom's mispronunciation of 'Ninus' in rehearsal (*Act 3 Scene 1*)

    i Does it have any effect on the outcome, in *Act 5 Scene 1*?

    ii From Quince's own performance before the Duke, what are his own shortcomings?

2 **a** Francis Flute is probably the youngest of the tradesmen. How can we deduce this from what he says in *Act 1 Scene 2*?

b Flute is apparently Bottom's most ardent admirer. Illustrate this from his words in *Act 4 Scene 2*.

c What evidence is there in *Act 4 Scene 2* that Flute's vocabulary is better than that of his senior colleagues?

3 **a** Tom Snout the tinker says very little in *Act 1 Scene 2*. Look up the part he is given by Peter Quince. What do you notice about it?

b In the rehearsal scene, *Act 3 Scene 1*, he makes several contributions to the discussion. What kind of man does he seem to be?

4 Of all the tradesmen Snug is the one who admits to his educational weakness.

a Find the line in *Act 1 Scene 2* which reveals it.

b If Bottom had not intervened, his weakness would never have been put to the test.

    i Check what Bottom recommends in *Act 3 Scene 1*

and

ii check whether Snout carries out the recommendations faithfully in *Act 5 Scene 1*.

5   Robin Starveling, first cast as Thisbe's mother in the
tradesmen's play, plays Moonshine in the actual
production.

a How does this second part come to exist?

b In *Act 5 Scene 1*, Starveling makes two attempts to say his
lines according to the script. Look up his third attempt
and say what can be deduced about his feelings by this
time.

6   Shakespeare's choice of names for the tradesmen has comic
purpose. Identify the surname of each from the following definitions:

a a nose or spout of kettle

b the spool on which yarn is wound

c tight, like a well-made wood joint

d a skinny man, such as tailors were thought to be

e a wedge of wood

f an instrument with a high pitch

The fairies

Oberon and Titania

1   In *Act 2 Scene 1*, Puck tells us that the fairy king and fairy
queen have quarrelled over 'a lovely boy stolen from an
Indian king'.

a Why does Oberon want to have him?

b Why does Titania want to keep him?

2   Next, Oberon and Titania engage in a verbal battle: the kind
that Puck says makes 'all their elves for fear/Creep into
acorn cups and hide them there'.

a In Round One,

    i what adjective does Oberon use to describe Titania, and why does he believe he is justified in using it?

    ii What adjective does Titania use to describe Oberon, and who else uses the same one in the same scene?

b In Round Two Titania accuses Oberon of unfaithfulness.

    i What is her first example of it?

    ii What is her second?

    iii What is Oberon's response?

c In Round Three, Titania describes the catastrophic effect of their quarrel on the weather.

    i List her catalogue of natural disasters

    ii Say whether you agree or disagree with Oberon's retort 'Do you amend it then, it lies in you'.

3 Oberon's use of magic is intended as a solution to his own domestic dispute, and the problems of certain young Athenians.

a What mistake does he make in giving Puck instructions?

b What consequences follow?

4 Titania is made to love Bottom, complete with his ass's head.

a Do you agree or disagree that Titania never loses her dignity?

b Do you agree or disagree that Shakespeare is successful in maintaining Titania's fairy-like characteristics even when she is doting on 'the shallowest thick-skin of that barren sort'?

c When Oberon sees them together in *Act 4 Scene 1*, he speaks of 'this sweet sight' (not this 'absurd' one) and is moved to pity (rather than to laughter). Explain why.

Puck

1 Puck is a mischievous spirit, given to practical jokes.

   a A fairy in *Act 2 Scene 1* addresses him first in a general way. What is the phrase used, and what does it imply?

   b On closer acquaintance, the fairy recognises Puck and reveals that he is known by other names. What are they?

   c The fairy identifies several of Puck's typical jokes. Puck confesses to many more. List them all.

2 Puck is Oberon's servant.

   a How do we know from evidence in *Act 2 Scene 1* that they work closely together, but that Oberon has greater powers?

   b What remarkable power does Puck claim when challenged to be quick in carrying out his master's orders?

3 Look up Puck's activities in *Act 3*.

   a Which speeches in *Scene 1* show that he enjoys making mischief?

   b Which speech in *Scene 2*

     i describes in detail the results of his tricks on the tradesmen

     ii shows that he chose Bottom to maximise the effect of his practical joke?

   c Which speeches in *Scene 2* show

     i that Puck makes mistakes, and sometimes deliberately

     ii that he is scornful of human beings, especially those in love

     iii that he has a taste for the absurd, and enjoys stirring up trouble

     iv that he has no kinship with the spirits of darkness?

4 Puck's final appearance in *Act 5 Scene 1* rounds off the play.

   a How does he reiterate the point that he belongs to the benevolent forces of night, not the sinister ones?

   b How, in his final speech, does Puck bring the audience from the world of imagination to the real world?

5 Show the ways in which Puck binds together the separate strands in *A Midsummer Night's Dream* by his involvement with

   a Oberon and Titania

   b the lovers

   c the tradesmen

   d Theseus and Hippolyta.

Structure

A Midsummer Night's Dream comprises four separate stories which are interwoven into a whole during the course of the play:

A The story of Theseus and Hippolyta and their marriage

B The story of Lysander, Demetrius, Helena and Hermia and their tangled love affairs

C The story of the Athenian tradesmen and their play

D The story of Oberon and Titania and their quarrel.

1 All four plots involve a conflict, past or present.

    a What was the conflict in the Theseus/Hippolyta relationship prior to the action of the play, and how was it resolved?

    b i What is the initial conflict in the story of the lovers?

        ii What other conflicts ensue, and how are they resolved?

    c What conflict is there in the play of *Pyramus and Thisbe*, and what is its outcome?

    d What conflict is there between Oberon and Titania, and who is the victor?

2   **a** i Which of the four stories is the framework for the other three?

        ii Which of the four stories requires the greatest use of the imagination?

        iii Which of the four stories is mainly in prose?

        iv Which of the four stories has the major romantic interest?

    b Shakespeare gives the last words in the play to a character from Story D. Why is this artistically appropriate?

3   **a** Identify the Acts and Scenes in which these stories first

connect with each other.
Story A to Story C
Story B to Story D
Story C to Story A
Story D to Story B

b In which Act are all four stories first brought together?

4   Each story is connected with at least one other story. Work out which stories are interrelated.

5   The action of the play begins in Athens, moves to a nearby wood, and then returns to Athens.

a In which setting is day predominant, and in which night?

b In which setting is the plot set in motion, and also resolved?

c In which setting is fact predominant, and in which fantasy?

Themes

Love

The central theme of *A Midsummer Night's Dream* is love, and its eventual consummation in marriage.

1 The mature love between Theseus and Hippolyta is introduced at the beginning of the play, and their marriage ends it.

 a What evidence is there in *Act 1 Scene 1* that they are in control of their passions?

 b What evidence is there that they have been in conflict, but that the conflict has been resolved to their mutual satisfaction?

 c i What evidence is there at the beginning of *Act 5 Scene 1* that Theseus is sceptical of young lovers and their lack of reason?

   ii What decision has Theseus already made in *Act 4 Scene 1*, however, which shows that he understands and sympathises with their problems?

2 In contrast, there is the theme of young love, as exemplified by Lysander, Demetrius, Helena and Hermia.

 a Which character in *Act 1 Scene 1* represents an obstacle to happiness with which mature love is not concerned?

 b When young love is thwarted, what is the remedy proposed in *Act 1 Scene 1*, and carried out in *Act 2 Scene 2*?

 c What examples does Lysander give in *Act 1 Scene 1* of the course of true love never running smooth?

 d i Which of the four lovers has a history of inconstancy?

   ii How is it cured?

e What is Helena's analysis of love, as stated towards the end of *Act 1 Scene 1*?

f What is the attitude of Egeus to young love, as demonstrated by his opening address to Theseus in *Act 1 Scene 1*?

g What is Bottom's view of love affairs, as stated in *Act 3 Scene 1*?

h What is Puck's pronouncement on lovers' vows, as stated in *Act 3 Scene 2*?

i How does the play of *Pyramus and Thisbe* relate in its comic way to the theme of young love?

3 Discord in love is represented in the story of Oberon and Titania. Analyse their quarrel in *Act 2 Scene 1*.

a What is Oberon's assumption about his role in their marriage?

b What is Titania's complaint about his behaviour?

c Whose authority prevails in the end?

Friendship

4 A related theme is friendship. Give details of the friendship between
  i Helena and Hermia in childhood (*Act 3 Scene 2*)
  ii Titania and her votaress (*Act 2 Scene 1*)
  iii Bottom and his fellow tradesmen (*Act 4 Scene 2*)
  iv The fairies and Duke Theseus (*Act 5 Scene 1*)

Illusion and reality

5 Another important theme in the play is illusion, the difficulty of distinguishing between imagination and reality.

a Which speech in *Act 2 Scene 2* best illustrates Lysander's delusion after Puck has applied the magic charm?

b Which speech in *Act 3 Scene 2* best illustrates Demetrius's delusion after Oberon's intervention?

c Which speech in *Act 3 Scene 1* typifies Titania's delusions?

d Which phrase of Puck's in *Act 3 Scene 2*, repeated four times in four lines, expresses his mischievous pleasure in deluding his victims?

e How do the tradesmen show

    i in their discussions during rehearsals (*Act 1 Scene 2, Act 3 Scene 1*)

    ii in the performance of *Pyramus and Thisbe* (*Act 5 Scene 1*)

that they underestimate the ability of their audience to distinguish between illusion and reality?

f What have Theseus and Hippolyta to say about illusion and reality at the beginning of *Act 5 Scene 1*?

g What has Puck to say about it in his final speech?

6 Counterpointing the theme of illusion and reality, there is repeated reference to the eyes: sight is obscured (as in the fog ordered by Oberon in *Act 3 Scene 2*), or rendered useless (as Hermia points out in searching for Lysander in the dark, *Act 3 Scene 2*). Find as many references to eyes as you can in *Act 1 Scene 1, Act 2 Scene 2, Act 3 Scene 1, Act 3 Scene 2, Act 4 Scene 1* and *Act 5 Scene 1*, and say how they illustrate the importance of perception in the play.

Atmosphere, imagery and setting

1 The play's title is *A Midsummer Night's Dream*. The word 'dream' occurs as early as the second speech of the play, and as late as the final one. Find as many references to sleeping and dreaming as you can – at least one from each Act – and say how they combine to establish the play's atmosphere.

2 **a** The moon is mentioned in the first few lines of the play and again frequently until *Act 3 Scene 2*. Collect as many examples as you can find and say how these references would have been of particular help to an Elizabethan audience at *The Globe*.

   b What is different about the moon when it reappears as a feature of the play in *Act 5 Scene 1*?

   c What is the final reference to the moon, and how does it fit in with the play's preoccupation with dreams and magic?

3 Although the play is set in and around Athens, it is rich in references to Elizabethan England, its people and its countryside.

   a Read the speeches of Puck and the fairy in *Act 2 Scene 1*. Identify
       i references to natural features of the countryside
       ii references to the common people and their activities.

   b What further details does Titania subsequently provide?

   c In which speech does Oberon describe the lushness of the rural scene?

4 **a** The fairies sing a protective lullaby in *Act 2 Scene 2*. List the small creatures they wish to frighten away.

   b Oberon's incantation in the same scene involves the presence of animals that are large and threatening. Identify them.

   c In Puck's mischievous interruption of the rehearsal in *Act 3 Scene 1* he makes harsh, discordant references to nature. What are they?

   d How does Bottom add to our knowledge of English birds in the song he sings to keep up his spirits? How are the dialogues between Bottom and Titania in *Act 3 Scene 1* and *Act 4 Scene 1* enriched by a sense of nature's plenty?

5   How do the lovers in the quarrel scene (*Act 3 Scene 1*) use the things of nature to convey their angry feelings?

6   Puck in *Act 3 Scene 2* and Theseus in *Act 4 Scene 1* refer to rural pursuits: the former those of country people, the latter of the gentry. Trace the references and say how they differ in purpose.

Music and dance

A Midsummer Night's Dream is a lyrical play: its poetry is mostly spoken, but sometimes it is sung and there are several dance sequences.

1   Except in *Act 5 Scene 1*, when they comment on the performance of *Pyramus and Thisbe*, Theseus and Hippolyta speak in blank verse – the iambic pentameter of ten syllables to the line. Choose one speech by Theseus in *Act 1 Scene 1* and one by Hippolyta in *Act 4 Scene 1*, and show how the form of their speech conveys a sense of dignity.

2   **a** The lovers also speak in blank verse, especially in formal situations. Find a typical example for each.

      b The lovers occasionally speak in rhymed couplets; choose examples of this from *Acts 1, 2 and 3* that seem to you to be in harmony with the romantic situation.

3   **a** Oberon and Titania speak in blank verse when they quarrel in *Act 2 Scene 1*. Why is this appropriate?

      b Sometimes Oberon speaks in short couplets. Find an example in *Act 2 Scene 2* and say why it is effective for its particular purpose.

      c Oberon and Puck deliver several incantations when using the magic love-juice. All are in short rhymed couplets except one. Find them.

d Read the first fairy's speech at the beginning of *Act 2 Scene 1*. How does its verse pattern vividly convey the lightness, speed, beauty and benevolence of this supernatural character?

e Find similar examples of fairy-like lyricism in Puck's speeches (*Acts 2, 3 and 4*).

f The fairies sing a lullaby in *Act 2 Scene 2*. How does
  i this fit in with the requirements of the plot
  ii add to the supernatural atmosphere?

g The fairies sing and dance at the end of the play.
  i How does this help the play in performance
  ii prepare the audience for Puck's concluding remarks?

h Music and dancing are natural ritual activities of the fairies. Find examples in *Act 2 Scene 1, Act 2 Scene 2, Act 4 Scene 1* and *Act 5 Scene 1*.

4 In *Act 5 Scene 1* the tradesmen dance a Bergomask, which is a rough kind of rustic dance. Some producers burlesque it, while others take it seriously. Make out a case for each interpretation and say which you prefer.

5 Several speeches in *A Midsummer Night's Dream* are so lyrical that they have a music of their own, or have attracted the attention of composers. Choose two which you think might well be set to music.

Close reading

Read the original Shakespeare and (if necessary) the modern version to gain an understanding of the speeches and extracts below. Then concentrate entirely on the original in answering the questions.

1 *How happy some o'er other some can be* (*Act 1 Scene 1*)

   a Helena's lament on the subject of unrequited love is a soliloquy. She thinks aloud, so we can see how she arrives at a point of decision. Where does thought end and action begin?

   b i What is similar about the construction of the first line and the fourth?

      ii What is achieved by this poetic device?

   c The soliloquy is in rhyming couplets. What effect has this on the flow of Helena's ideas?

   d i How often does Helena refer to eyes?

      ii Explain the relationship of eyes, sight and seeing to the theme of the play as a whole.

   e Several of Cupid's characteristics are referred to here.

      i What are they?

      ii What significance have they, according to Helena?

      iii Which two spell danger?

   f How does the word 'hailed' in line 246 lead to a sequence of metaphors explaining Demetrius's unfaithfulness?

2 *Over hill, over dale* (*Act 2 Scene 1*)

   a How does verse form suggest the light and airy qualities of a delicate fairy, in sharp contrast with the 'mortal grossness' of the tradesmen in the previous scene?

   b The fairy's duty is to collect dew. How does this further add to your imaginative understanding of fairy scale?

    c The dew has two uses: what are they?

    d How do these uses help to suggest that the fairy queen rules over a diminutive world of natural beauty?

    e Which words in the fairy's speech suggest the richness of nature's beauty?

    f Puck is called 'thou lob of spirits'

        i Why does 'lob' stand out in contrast with the rest of the fairy's speech and

       ii does the word help to distinguish between the workstyles of the two spirits?

3 *Thou speak'st aright/I am that merry wanderer of the night (Act 2 Scene 1)*

    a The fairy has already identified Puck correctly, and given examples to show that he is a 'shrewd and knavish sprite'. What three further jests does Puck boast of here?

    b One talent he claims is practised later in the play. What is it, and in which Act and Scene does Puck demonstrate his skill?

    c Which of Puck's mischievous acts show he has no respect for old age?

    d Which of them shows he has an earthy sense of humour?

    e Which of them shows

        i that he likes his jokes to be widely enjoyed

       ii that he is appreciated by rustic people?

    f Which lines spoken by Puck to Oberon in *Act 3 Scene 2* are further evidence that he regards mischief-making as a sport?

4 *These are the forgeries of jealousy (Act 2 Scene 1)*

    a To what is Titania referring in the first line?

    b Titania gives seven examples of places where fairies like to dance. Identify them.

    c Next, she gives three instances of inclement weather. What are they?

d Continuing, she lists the natural disasters that have happened as a consequence.

    i How have farmers been affected?

    ii How have villagers been affected?

    iii How have householders been affected?

e What two examples does Titania give of unseasonal occurrences?

f In the last three lines of the speech, Titania stresses three words. What are they?

5 *That very time I saw, but thou couldst not* (*Act 2 Scene 1*)

This is Oberon's account of how he came to possess the potent love-juice which makes 'or man or woman madly dote/Upon the next live creature that it sees'. It is also an elaborate compliment to Elizabeth I, 'the virgin queen'. Examine the passage carefully and explain why she would be flattered by it (as many scholars believe) when it was first acted before her, probably on the occasion of a marriage between two of her noble subjects.

6 *I know a bank whereon the wild thyme blows* (*Act 2 Scene 1*)

a The first part of Oberon's speech is memorable for its lush catalogue of English flowers amongst which, he says, Titania sometimes sleeps. List them.

b Which words suggest the bank is subject to gentle breezes?

c Which words suggest the richness of the growth?

d Which word hints at fragrance?

e Which line tells us that Titania's sleep follows from a pleasurable activity that is characteristic of her?

f How does reference to the snake introduce colour to his description?

g How does reference to the snake also assist in understanding fairy size?

h Which line is in sharp contrast with the others, proving the power of Oberon's love-juice?

i The second part of the speech is businesslike. How is this reflected in the movement of the verse?

7 *Oh Helen, goddess, nymph, perfect divine* (*Act 3 Scene 2*)

a The Elizabethan romantic lover was given to excessive and elaborate compliments. In line one, at what level does Demetrius pitch his Helen-worship?

b Demetrius selects three of Helena's features to praise: what (significantly) is the first, and how does he achieve the appropriate extravagance in his comparison?

c What is the second, and how flattering is the metaphor?

d What is the third? Explain the wider dimensions involved in establishing it as 'this princess of pure white, this seal of bliss'.

8 *Lo, she is one of this confederacy* (*Act 3 Scene 2*)

a Helena's appeal is a passionate one, intended to move her listeners to pity. At what point do her lines cease to rhyme, and why?

b From the point where blank verse begins, how many rhetorical questions does she ask, and how does she inject an emotional quality into her sentence-structure?

c In elaborating her appeal, Helena develops the idea of two people living and working as one.

   i How does the repetition of key words 'one', 'both' and 'our' suggest a harmony and unity in their longstanding friendship?

   ii How does she strengthen her case by the use of the extended simile of the 'double cherry'?

   iii Explain her image 'like coats in heraldry, due but to one and crowned with one crest'. (If possible, find a real-life example, or draw one.)

d Helena ends her 'passionate words' by a return to the rhetorical question and a further use of repetition.

Identify the devices, and explain how they help to achieve an effective climax.

9 *When my cue comes, call me, and I will answer* (*Act 4 Scene 1*)

  a How do Bottom's first words on awakening from Oberon's spell typify
    i his commitment to the play and
    ii his total self-confidence?

  b How many times does he use the personal pronoun 'I', and what does this suggest about his thought-patterns?

  c Which word does Bottom use which an audience finds funny because they know more than he does?

  d i In trying to explain the mystery of his amazing dream, Bottom mixes up the senses five times. Identify each.
    ii What other examples of this kind of confusion can you find in the scenes in which he appears?

  e i What is amusing about the title of the proposed ballad?
    ii What is amusing about Bottom's plans for its performance?

10 *More strange than true. I never may believe* (*Act 5 Scene 1*)

  a Theseus begins by declaring he is a sceptic. About what?
  b How does he make his point in terms of hot and cold?
  c Lunatics, lovers and poets have one faculty in common, he says. What is it?
  d i How does the madman demonstrate his possession of this faculty?
    ii How does the lover?
    iii How does the poet?

  e The madman, the lover and the poet may share this common faculty, but only the poet (says Theseus) takes matters a stage further. What is the unique gift that the poet alone possesses?

    f What examples does Theseus give of the power of the imagination?

11   *If we offend, it is with our good will (Act 5 Scene 1)*

Peter Quince reads the Prologue with scant regard for punctuation, thus altering the meaning of his script. Write out the speech as you think its author intended.

12   *If we shadows have offended (Act 5 Scene 1)*

    a Puck remains after the fairies and the mortals have left the stage, and he is speaking here to the audience on behalf of 'we shadows'. 'Shadows' can mean 'fairies', (Oberon is 'king of shadows' in *Act 3 Scene 2*), or 'actors', (Theseus says of players 'the best in this kind are shadows' in *Act 5 Scene 1*). He can mean either, or both. What would your own interpretation be?

    b He offers excuses for 'this weak and idle theme'. Why might the play be subject to this kind of harsh criticism?

    c How are his excuses consistent with the title of the play?

    d How does he plead for tolerance in a witty way?

    e 'The serpent's tongue' is Puck's way of referring to an audience's classic response to a bad play. What is the simple word for it today?

    f What is the double meaning of 'give me your hands, if we be friends'?

Textual questions

The following are typical of the kind of examination questions set by the major examining boards:

1 How relevant is the title of the play to the adventures in the wood of *either* the young lovers *or* Bottom?

2 How important are the parallels between the mortals Theseus and Hippolyta and the fairies Oberon and Titania?

3 Give an account of the scene which begins with the complaint of Egeus to Theseus and ends with Helena's decision to tell Demetrius of the flight of Lysander and Hermia. Explain how this establishes the relationship between the young lovers, and starts the action of the play.

4 Show the ways in which Shakespeare portrays love in *A Midsummer Night's Dream*.

5 'Bottom and Quince are comic characters, but they are people we can believe in and like'. Do you agree?

6 'Although Theseus is not a character who interests us, his role is vital to the action of the play'. Comment on this opinion.

7 'Shrewd and knavish sprite'. Is this an apt description of Puck?

8 'The dramatic interest of *A Midsummer Night's Dream* is achieved by a skilful mingling of three very different groups: courtiers, artisans and fairies'. How far do you think this is true?

9 '*A Midsummer Night's Dream* has a dream-like quality in terms of its characters and its setting, which is befitting to a play of this name'. Explain and illustrate.

10 How does the mixture of comedy and seriousness make the character of Bottom outstanding amongst the Athenian working men?

11 Choose (i) a scene in the wood, or a part of a scene, in which two or more of the lovers appear and (ii) a scene involving Oberon and Titania. Write a detailed account of the two scenes you have chosen so as to illustrate the characters of those involved.

12 Describe in detail the distresses suffered by the four Athenian lovers from the time when Puck applies the love-juice to Lysander's eyes to the time when all four fall asleep.

13 'Lord, what fools these mortals be'. Are Oberon and Titania above such foolishness?

14 'Lord, what fools these mortals be'. To what extent do you think the behaviour of (i) the lovers and (ii) the workmen justifies this mocking comment?

15 Describe in some detail the performance of *Pyramus and Thisbe* at the end of the play. What do you think of the behaviour of the courtly audience?

16 Compare Hermia with Helena. Have you found one more interesting than the other? If so, give reasons.

17 Write full accounts of any two scenes in which the Athenian workpeople are involved, so as to bring out (i) the individual characteristics of the participants and (ii) their comic qualities.

18 What opinion of Bottom is held (i) by himself and (ii) by other characters in the play?

19 What part does nature play in the language of *A Midsummer Night's Dream*?

20 How great a significance is the theme of change and transformation in *A Midsummer Night's Dream*?

One-word-answer quiz

1 What was Bottom's trade?

2 What was his christian name?

3 Who was 'King of shadows'?

4 Whose cue was 'Deceiving me'?

5 In and around which city does the play take place?

6 Who had the consent of Egeus to marry Hermia?

7 What was the name of Helena's father?

8 What course, according to Lysander, never did run smooth?

9 What did the wisest aunt cry as she fell off the three-legged stool?

10 After the performance of *Pyramus and Thisbe*, what entertainment did Theseus choose?

11 Whose singing caused the rude sea to grow civil?

12 How many leagues from Athens was the house of Lysander's aunt?

13 How many leagues from Athens was the wood?

14 For how long does Theseus say the wedding celebrations should continue?

15 Whose job was it 'to sweep the dust behind the door'?

16 What was the christian name of Quince the carpenter?

17 Oberon's magic spell is removed from all his victims but one. Name him.

18 What flowers does Titania place in Bottom's 'sleek smooth beard'?

19 Who sees 'more devils than vast hell can hold', according to Theseus?

20 How many days and nights did Theseus and Hippolyta have to wait for their wedding day?

21 How many hours had to be filled in on the wedding day between 'after-supper and bedtime'?

22 What was the name of Theseus's entertainments manager?

23 Who played Thisbe in the play performed before the Duke?

24 Whose tomb was to be the meeting place of Pyramus and Thisbe?

25 Which of the tradesmen was 'slow of study'?

26 Who sometimes slept on a bank 'whereon the wild thyme blows'?

27 Of what tribe was Hippolyta the queen?

28 Who was a vixen when she went to school?

29 Who was the darker – Hermia or Helena?

30 Who was the taller – Hermia or Helena?

31 Who spoke the Prologue to the play of *Pyramus and Thisbe*?

32 Who is called 'thou lob of spirits'?

33 Who was the bellows-mender?

34 By what did Pyramus and Thisbe meet, as well as Oberon and Titania?

35 What other name was Robin Goodfellow known by?

36 Whose kindred had made Bottom's eyes water?

37 Who was asked to 'be further off'?

38 Which of the Athenian tradesmen was a tinker?

39 'This fellow doth not stand upon points'. Which fellow?

40 What was the name of the flower from which Oberon extracted his magic juice?

41 Which fairy was instructed to scratch Bottom's head?

42 Who, according to Theseus, 'sees Helen's beauty in a brow of Egypt'?

43 What kind of hounds did Theseus own?

44 Who was 'a lover that kills himself most gallant for love'?

45 How much per day did Flute think Bottom deserved as a pension?

46 With what was the nine-men's morris filled, according to Titania?

47 In how many minutes could Puck put a girdle round the earth?

48 What, according to Bottom 'hath no fellow'?

49 What was the nationality of the 'little changeling boy'?

50 What trade did Starveling follow?

What's missing?

Complete the following:

1 Thou speak'st aright; I am that . . .
2 I know a bank . . .
3 To show our simple skill, / That is the . . .
4 If we shadows have offended . . .
5 Lord, what fools . . .
6 The cowslips tall her pensioners be . . .
7 Merry and tragical? Tedious and brief? That is . . .
8 The raging rocks / And shivering shocks / Shall . . .
9 Love, therefore, and tongue-tied simplicity . . .
10 Either I mistake your shape and making quite Or else . . .
11 What thou seest when thou dost wake / Do it . . .
12 Be advised, fair maid. To you your father should be . . .
13 If you were men, as men you are in show, / You . . .
14 Thus hath he lost sixpence a day during his life; . . .
15 I am not yet so low / But that . . .
16 Jack shall have Jill; / Naught shall go ill; / The man . . .
17 These are the . . . of jealousy.
18 We will, fair queen, up to the mountain's top, / And . . .
19 I see a voice; now will I to the chink, / To . . .
20 Love looks not with the eyes, but with . . .
21 These things seem small and indistinguishable, / Like . . .
22 In this same interlude, it doth befall / That I . . .
23 She was a vixen when she went to school / And though . . .
24 Cupid is a knavish lad, / Thus to . . .
25 Marry, our play is ' . . . '
26 I'll put a girdle round about the earth . . .

27 The poet's eye, in fine frenzy rolling / Doth . . .

28 But oh, methinks how slow / This old moon wanes! . . .

29 The nine-men's morris is filled up with mud / And . . .

30 I do wander everywhere . . .

31 The course of true love . . .

32 Most radiant Pyramus, most lily-white of hue, / Of colour . . .

33 Music, ho music, such as . . .

34 The lunatic, the lover and the poet . . .

35 I will roar, that I will make the Duke say: ' . . . '

36 For never anything can be amiss / When . . .

37 I will get Peter Quince to write a ballad of this dream; it shall be called . . .

38 I am sent with broom before / To . . .

39 Yet marked I where the bolt of Cupid fell: / It fell upon . . .

40 Now am I dead, / Now am I fled, / My soul is in the sky . . .

41 Two lovely berries, moulded on one stem; / So . . .

42 Turn melancholy forth to . . .

43 Then fate o'errules, that, one man holding troth . . .

44 Earthlier happy is the rose distilled / Than that which . . .

45 His speech was like a tangled chain: nothing impaired . . .

46 I must to the barbers, monsieur, for methinks . . .

47 One turf shall serve as pillow for us both: . . .

48 I go, I go, look how I go / Swifter than . . .

49 A calendar, a calendar; look in the almanac; . . .

50 Oh then, what graces in my love do dwell / That he hath turned . . .

More plays in the
SHAKESPEARE MADE EASY
series

All these plays are available from your bookshop or newsagent or you can order them direct. Just tick the title you want and complete the order form below.

— MACBETH	£2.95
— ROMEO AND JULIET	£2.95
— THE MERCHANT OF VENICE	£2.95
— JULIUS CAESAR	£2.95
— HENRY IV PART ONE	£2.95
— A MIDSUMMER NIGHT'S DREAM	£2.95
— TWELFTH NIGHT	£2.95
— THE TEMPEST	£2.95
— HAMLET	£2.95
— KING LEAR	£2.95

H E D Books, BOOKSERVICE BY POST, PO BOX 17, Canvey Island, SS8 8HZ

Please enclose a cheque or postal order made out to H E D Books for the amount due plus 40p per book for postage and packing for orders within the UK. Orders for Western Europe add £1.45 per book.

Please print clearly

Name _____

Address _____

_____

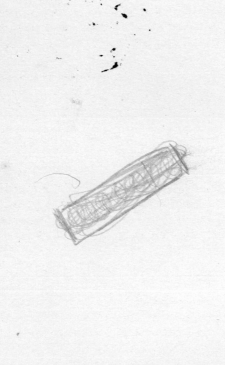